M000296609

Good Places for All

CALVIN SHORTS

A series published by the Calvin Press
Titles in the Calvin Shorts Series:

Good Places for All

Mark D. Bjelland

Grand Rapids, MI • calvin.edu/press

Copyright © 2019 Mark D. Bjelland

All rights reserved. No part of this publication may be reproduced, stored in a retrieval system, or transmitted, in any form or by any means, electronic, mechanical, photocopying, recording, or otherwise without the prior written permission of the publisher.

Published 2019 by The Calvin Press
3201 Burton St. SE
Grand Rapids, MI 49546

Unless otherwise noted, Scripture quotations are from the Holy Bible, New International Version®. NIV®. Copyright © 1973, 1978, 1984, 2011 by Biblica, Inc.™ Used by permission of Zondervan. All rights reserved worldwide. www.zondervan.com. The "NIV" and "New International Version" are trademarks registered in the United States Patent and Trademark Office by Biblica, Inc.™

Scripture quotations labeled CJB are from the Complete Jewish Bible. Copyright © 1998 by David H. Stern. All rights reserved.

Publisher's Cataloging-in-Publication Data

Names: Bjelland, Mark D., author.
Title: Good places for all / Mark D. Bjelland.
Series: Calvin Shorts.
Description: Grand Rapids, MI: The Calvin Press, 2019.
Identifiers: LCCN 2019953496 | ISBN 978-1-937555-41-2 (pbk.)
  | 978-1-937555-42-9 (ebook)
Subjects: LCSH City planning—United States. | Cities and towns—
  Religious aspects. | City planning—Religious aspects. | Neighborhoods.
  Urban renewal—United States. | Community development, Urban—
  United States. | Community development—Religious aspects—
  Christianity. | Sustainable development—United States. | BISAC
  POLITICAL SCIENCE / Public Policy / City Planning & Urban
  Development | SOCIAL SCIENCE / Sociology / Urban | RELIGION /
  Christian Living / Social Issues
Classification: LCC BV625 .B54 2019 | DDC 267/.13--dc23

Cover design: Robert Alderink
Interior design and typeset: Katherine Lloyd, The DESK

The Calvin Press has no responsibility for the persistence or accuracy of URLs for external or third-party internet websites referred to in this publication and does not guarantee that any content on such websites is, or will remain, accurate or appropriate.

Contents

Series Editor's Foreword

Midway along the journey of our life
I woke to find myself in some dark woods,
For I had wandered off from the straight path.

So begins *The Divine Comedy*, a classic meditation on the Christian life, written by Dante Alighieri in the fourteenth century.

Dante's three images—a journey, a dark forest, and a perplexed pilgrim—still feel familiar today, don't they?

We can readily imagine our own lives as a series of journeys: not just the big journey from birth to death, but also all the little trips from home to school, from school to job, from place to place, from old friends to new. In fact, we often feel we are simultaneously on multiple journeys that tug us in diverse and sometimes opposing directions. We recognize those dark woods from fairy tales and nightmares and the all-too-real conundrums that crowd our everyday lives. No wonder we frequently feel perplexed. We wake up shaking our heads, unsure if we know how to live wisely today or tomorrow or next week.

This series has in mind just such perplexed pilgrims. Each book invites you, the reader, to walk alongside experienced guides who will help you understand the contours of the road as well as the surrounding landscape. They will cut back the underbrush, untangle myths and misconceptions, and suggest ways to move forward.

And they will do it in books intended to be read in an evening or during a flight. Calvin Shorts are designed not just for perplexed pilgrims but also for busy ones. We live in a complex and changing world. We need nimble ways to acquire knowledge, skills, and wisdom. These books are one way to meet those needs.

John Calvin, after whom this series is named, recognized our pilgrim condition. "We are always on the road," he said, and although this road, this life, is full of perplexities, it is also "a gift of divine kindness which is not to be refused." Calvin Shorts takes as its starting point this claim that we are called to live well in a world that is both gift and challenge.

In *The Divine Comedy*, Dante's guide is Virgil, a wise but not omniscient mentor. So, too, the authors in the Calvin Shorts series don't pretend to know it all. They, like you and me, are pilgrims. And they invite us to walk with them as together we seek to live more faithfully in this world that belongs to God.

Susan M. Felch
Executive Editor
The Calvin Press

Additional Resources

Additional online resources for *Good Places for All* may be available at www.calvin.edu/press.

Additional information, references, and citations are included in the notes at the end of this book. Rather than using footnote numbers, the comments are keyed to phrases and page numbers.

Good Places for All is underwritten by the Calvin Institute of Christian Worship.

Acknowledgments

I wish to express my gratitude to those whose work made this book possible: Michaela Osborne, who managed the publication process, and Susan Felch, who was an inspiring, insightful, and patient editor. I owe a great debt to the three readers who made incredibly helpful suggestions on earlier drafts: Rev. Barbara Sartorius Bjelland, Dr. Steve Holloway of the Department of Geography at the University of Georgia, and Jan van der Woerd of the Inner City Christian Federation. I would also like to acknowledge those students and professors who have shared courses and conversations that have shaped and sharpened my thinking: John S. Adams, LisaBeth Barajas, Christina Bohnet, Alicia Bradshaw, Susan Bratton, Janaya Crevier, John Mason, Roger Miller, Evalyn Pelfrey, Noah Schumerth, Rylan Shewmaker, and Loren Wilkinson.

Our Place Matters

1

He brought us to this place and gave us this land,
a land flowing with milk and honey.

—DEUTERONOMY 26:9

PLACES SHAPE US

Where did you grow up?

Before you begin to read this book, take a bit of time to think about your childhood home. What did your house look like? Who were your neighbors? Where was your school and your church? What were your favorite places? Would you describe your neighborhood as rural? urban? suburban?

My parents grew up on midwestern farms, my brother and I in the heart of Minneapolis. That difference created an immense gulf in who we are and how we see the world. When it comes time to choose a vacation spot or restaurant, we are literally coming from different places. My brother and I thrive on density, diversity, and the sensory overload of the city. My parents love sleepy small towns where everyone knows your name and what you'll order for dinner. They like living under wide prairie skies and observing the rhythms of agricultural life.

Now think back to the answers you gave to the questions in the first paragraph. How did your childhood place or places shape the person you are today? As we go through life, our places leave imprints on us. Perhaps you've taken an online dialect quiz and have been asked how you pronounce certain words or identify certain objects. Do you say "toMAYto" or "toMAHto"? Do you say "firefly" or "lightning bug"? Our answers show how we carry our childhood places with us. But our places shape more than the way we speak. Our places shape our taken-for-granted sense of how things work and how they should be. Our places exert a powerful influence over our health, our outlook, our politics, our friend group, and much more. Places are more than the stage on which we play out the drama of our lives. Places are active players in that drama. We shape our places, and our places shape us.

PLACES AND WELL-BEING

Consider how your place affects your health. In the opening chapters of the Bible, we read that God planted a garden and placed Adam and Eve in it. We were made to dwell in a place of beauty and bounty. Being surrounded by trees, meadows, and flowers contributes to human well-being. Studies show that on average people who live near parks live longer and healthier lives. People who live beneath busy airport flight paths show increased blood pressure and cardiac ailments. All else being equal, people heal faster in hospital rooms with views of gardens or trees.

We tend to think of physical health as the result of personal choices. But some cities offer clean air to breathe and safe water to drink, while others do not. Pleasant parks and trails for running or biking encourage us to exercise. But it is difficult to get enough exercise if your neighborhood is unsafe or lacks sidewalks or trails. It is difficult to eat healthy when your neighborhood lacks affordable fresh food choices. Many struggling small towns and poor urban neighborhoods are classified as food deserts because they lack healthy food options. The effects of unhealthy places show up in wider waistlines and a higher frequency of diabetes, strokes, and related diseases. In short, places matter to our physical well-being.

Places also affect our social lives. Simple features of our physical environment affect our relationships. People are more likely to know their neighbors if the traffic is light in front of their house. Front porches and sidewalks promote sociability among neighbors.

Or consider what social scientists call the neighborhood effect. Where you grow up has a decisive influence on your schooling and job opportunities. Poor children face all kinds of disadvantages in life. But *where* children grow up poor also makes a huge difference. Imagine two young adults who grew up in different places but with identical family, racial, and economic backgrounds. It turns out, for example, that a black man in his mid-thirties who grew up in a low-income family in Chicago's northern suburb of Skokie makes, on average, $19,000 to $30,000 a year more than if he had grown up in the same low-income family inside the Chicago city limits. Sure, Chicago and Skokie have a different look and feel, but why would that make such a difference? Let's explore that question.

Our life chances are shaped by more than our family background and our personal decisions. Where we live, especially when we are young, determines our choice of friends and our fellow classmates in school. Our neighborhood determines whether we have access to good schools, parks, and after-school programs. When we reach adulthood, the region in which we live determines the types of job opportunities available to us. Children from low-income families, especially boys, are most affected by the neighborhood where they grow up. Distressed neighborhoods that are segregated by income and race and that lack good schools and two-parent families have the greatest negative effect. The longer a child lives in a distressed neighborhood, the stronger the negative effects they carry with them for the rest of their life. You can view the online Opportunity Atlas (www.opportunityatlas.org) to see the influence of where a person grows up on their chances of adult success.

SORTED PLACES

Because neighborhoods affect the opportunities we will or will not enjoy throughout our lives, the fact that our places are becoming increasingly segregated is a matter of concern. More and more, North Americans sort themselves out geographically, isolating themselves in places inhabited by people like themselves. We sort ourselves by race, income, age, family status, education, and even political outlook.

Residential segregation along racial lines has long undermined efforts at reconciliation. But now, with people both waiting longer to start families and living longer, our communities are more and more segregated by age and the presence or absence of children. While some suburbs are filled with child-rearing families, school-age children are a rarity in the hip urban neighborhoods of our largest cities. We also have "mature" communities where residents are required to be at least fifty-five years of age.

Our places also both reflect and shape our politics. Maps of election results provide shocking confirmation of how differently people think in different places. Studies of Canadian cities have found that political convictions even influence where people choose to live. The voting patterns of residents of walkable urban neighborhoods are on the opposite end of the political spectrum from those living in private, gated neighborhoods.

PLACE AND OUR EXPERIENCE OF THE WORLD

Because our places shape our daily routines and social interactions, they also shape our outlook and understanding of the world.

My early years were marked by divorce, frequent moves, and a stint in foster care before my mom remarried and we settled into one of Minneapolis's urban neighborhoods. Most of my friends also came from broken homes. But the place where I grew up was not just my house, street, or neighborhood. While New York City was facing bankruptcy in the mid-1970s, life in Minneapolis was pretty good. Sure, my mom dreamed of moving to the suburbs. True, subtle racial discrimination persisted in ways I didn't see. But Minneapolis's public schools were well funded, its public libraries were well stocked, and the air and water were clean. The city's public transit system got me to school, shopping, and my first job.

On top of that, Minneapolis's park system offered splendid recreational facilities, a dozen public beaches, and parkways linking it all together. When I reached the parkway, I could pedal my bike for thirty-five uninterrupted miles through a ribbon of parks encircling the city, its lakes, and its rivers. Minneapolis was spared the decline that hit other Midwest cities like Detroit and Cleveland. Minneapolis was a city that worked.

One reason why my hometown never declined much is that it belonged to a region whose politics focused on the common good. There was a strong emphasis on creating quality public spaces in order to foster a shared life and sense of community. There was also a long tradition of cooperation and resource sharing among Minneapolis, St. Paul, and their suburbs. The different communities pooled a portion of their tax revenues to equalize resources. Despite some early disadvantages, by age eighteen, I had a high school diploma and a good job, and I was ready for university. A religious conversion in my teens and encouragement from home, teachers, and youth leaders made a huge difference in my life, but so did growing up where I did. In fact, Minneapolis is ranked second among the country's top one hundred urban areas for giving poor children the opportunity for upward mobility.

LOOKING AHEAD

In this book, we are going to explore how to make our places better so all people can thrive. To do so, we need to consider not just our houses and neighborhoods but also the cities and regions in which those houses and neighborhoods are "placed." In the following chapters, we will discuss problems and possible solutions. But what it means to cultivate good places depends on one's context. Strategies for faithfully cultivating good places will be different in Phoenix, Arizona, than in Detroit, Michigan.

In chapter 2, we will unpack the concept of "place" that we have begun to look at in this first chapter. In chapter 3, we will explore the dividing lines that fragment communities, cities, and school districts. Chapter 4 evaluates the positives and negatives of these administrative dividing lines. Chapter 5 examines the shared spaces in our communities. We will look at parks, shopping districts, and other gathering places as well as the streets, sidewalks, and transit systems that connect them together. Chapter 6 delves into how we build neighborhoods and a movement called the New Urbanism. Chapter 7 argues for the importance of good housing for everyone and explores problems in our housing systems. Chapter 8 recognizes that Christians excel at showing hospitality in their own houses and encourages us to extend that hospitality so that everyone has a place to call home. Finally, in chapter 9, we will conclude with some practical ways to improve the places we live, work, and play.

The goal of this book is to guide our engagement with local politics, city planning, neighborhood associations, and real estate development. This is not a comprehensive how-to book for fixing our towns and cities. Rather, it is a reflection on community life that seeks to stretch our geographical imaginations so that we take better moral account of our lives. My hope is that this book will help followers of Jesus Christ better understand the place they inhabit and find ways to cultivate its common good.

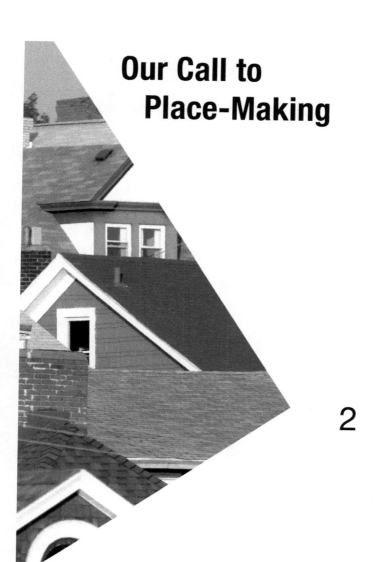

Our Call to Place-Making

2

ADONAI, God, took the person and put him
in the garden of 'Eden to cultivate and care for it.

GENESIS 2:15 CJB

WHAT IS PLACE?

Where are you right now? Perhaps you are reading by the
flickering lights of a fireplace. Or maybe you are sitting in
an airplane, gazing at the landscape below. Whether you
feel "at home" or "out of place," you are always situated in
a particular place. Because we have bodies, we are always
in a place.

Humans love to travel and experience new places. That
is why tourism is the world's largest industry. But we also
like to stay put. We put enormous effort into staying put by
gardening, remodeling our homes, and following the real
estate industry. Celebrity designers tell us how to create the
home of our dreams. Real estate professionals remind us
to choose a location wisely. Popular books promise to help
us choose the best places to live, learn to love our places,
or fix our places. Such books carry titles such as *The Power
of Place*; *Who's Your City?*; *Healing Spaces: The Science of
Place and Well-Being*; *Love Where You Live*; *This Is Where
You Belong*; *Welcome to Your World: How the Built Environment Shapes Our Lives*; and *Where We Want to Live*.

Places are spaces that have taken on meaning. Places are centers of human attention and care. Places matter because they bring together three essential elements for living: a material setting, social relationships, and meaning.

The material setting is the natural landscape as transformed by humans. Termites build colonies, and beavers build lodges. Humans cut trees and plant trees. We tend gardens and build roads, houses, and high-rises. Our material setting is a mixture of both human and natural elements.

A place without people is merely a space. That is why architects add fake people to their models and drawings. The social relationships formed when people inhabit a space are the second ingredient in place. These relationships are between neighbors, between businesses and their customers, and between residents and local institutions such as churches, sports clubs, parent-teacher associations, and other organizations.

Over time, as people dwell in a particular location, something new emerges. Layers of meaning accumulate, and a sense of place develops. Spaces becomes meaningful places, overlaid with experiences, feelings, memories, and stories. Thus, God's world is a rich mosaic of places—meaningful centers of human care—each one embodying a unique set of relationships among people and their environment.

OUR CALL TO CULTIVATION

To understand our identity as humans, it is helpful to start at the beginning, in the opening chapter of Genesis. The first thing to notice is that we humans were formed from the dust of the earth. The original Hebrew offers a play on words: God created the human (*Adam*) from the earth or soil (*adamah*). In English, if we think of humans as made from the humus or soil, we get a similar effect. Second, the human was placed by God in a garden. In short, to be human is to be an emplaced earth creature, *homo geographicus*.

The first chapter of Genesis continues with God's blessing on the first humans and instructions to "be fruitful and multiply and fill the earth and subdue it" (v. 28, NRSV). As humans, we are assigned the task of ruling over and filling the creation, ordering and developing its potentials. In essence, we are called to develop culture and make a world. In the second chapter of Genesis, God assigns the first humans the task of tilling and keeping the garden (v. 15, NRSV).

But how are we to reconcile our calls both to fill and till the earth and to rule over and care for the garden? The concept of cultivation, the term used in the Complete Jewish Bible translation of Genesis 2:15, offers a way forward. We are called to cultivate the earth, mixing our labor with the soil. A cultivator is a farm tool used to loosen and prepare the soil prior to planting. Then after the plants have germinated, the cultivator is used to uproot the weeds while sparing the crops. Because cultivation is about nurturing all that is good, we use the word not just for farming but also for improving life through education and training. Our calling, then, is to cultivate the good in the locations where God has placed us.

Continuing in the second chapter of Genesis, we read that "it is not good for the man to be alone" (v. 18). God set about remedying our loneliness by creating the first human community. From this passage, we see that to be fully human is to be in community. Just as the Triune God is a community of love, we humans are beings who need relationships. As Lutheran theologian Edgar Carlson expressed it, "We need each other in order to be ourselves."

Summing up the first chapters of Genesis, we are earth creatures and place dwellers. We are called to develop culture, care for the earth, build community, and cultivate what is good, true, and beautiful. Made in the image of God and placed on God's good earth, we are called to cultivate places that embody right, harmonious relationships between people, God, and the rest of creation. All three ingredients in our definition of place are present in the call to cultivate: a material setting to be shaped, relationships to be nurtured, and meaning to be embraced. As cultivators, we prepare the soil, protect the good, and uproot the weeds that intrude. We do this literally when we farm or garden. But we also do it when we cultivate the good in our homes, churches, neighborhoods, cities, and regions.

PLACE AS GOD'S GIFT

God's gift of place is a persistent biblical theme. The story of God's chosen people is intimately bound up with their relationship to the land of promise. The idea of a good and abundant place looms large in the call of Abraham, the desert sojourn, the entry into the Promised Land, and the return from Babylonian exile. The Promised Land represents belonging, rootedness, harmony, and flourishing. When God called Abraham, it was with the promise of a good land that would be given to his descendants. God's commands and promises were given so that his chosen people might "live and increase and may enter and possess the land the LORD promised" (Deut. 8:1). When the people obeyed, the land overflowed with abundance. When the people rebelled, the land suffered. When they were really bad, they were taken into exile.

During the exile in Babylon, God's promises to his chosen people seemed impossibly distant. Yet to the Hebrew people in exile, God's prophet Jeremiah offered instructions to "build houses and settle down; plant gardens and eat what they produce" (Jer. 29:5). Then the prophet added, "Also, seek the peace and prosperity of the city to which I have carried you into exile" (v. 7). In the midst of their exile, the Hebrew people were told by God's messenger to cultivate a good place. They were called to care about the place they inhabited and to seek its well-being.

Early Christians found inspiration in Jeremiah's words as they tried to figure out how to live their faith in a hostile, pagan society. Whenever it didn't conflict with their loyalty to Christ, they tried to be model citizens. They brought honor to Christ by the character, humility, and integrity of their lives. They outdid their pagan neighbors as they sought the welfare of the entire community. They cared for the sick and dying, even those who were not from their own group. Those Christians with financial means served as public benefactors, contributing to public works that promoted the well-being of the community. But a good community does not mean an ideal community.

IDEAL PLACES AND MESSY REALITIES

Thomas More's 1516 book *Utopia* coined a new word and sparked an ongoing fascination with ideal places. But the word *utopia* itself suggests the difficulty of achieving our ideals. Part of the word *utopia* comes from *topos*, the Greek word for "place." The prefix is trickier to decipher. In Greek, *eu* means "good," while *ou* means "non." Both are pronounced similarly, so utopia could mean either a good place or a non-place. Perhaps More was playfully suggesting that a utopia is both a perfect place and a non-existent one. That ambiguity is a helpful reminder that a perfectly good place is beyond our grasp.

Christ's incarnation and miracles affirm the value of earthly life. Christ's resurrection and the promise of the resurrection of our bodies further affirm God's care for bodily life. Biblical history begins in an abundant garden and ends in a heavenly garden city. The New Jerusalem will be filled with the presence of God and will be unimaginably good, beautiful, and true. In the meantime, we live as dual citizens. We seek the peace and prosperity of the actual, dirty, messy cities where we live, not just for our own sakes but for the good of everyone who lives there. We are called to cultivate good places. But for the truly good place, we must await God's unveiling of the New Jerusalem.

PLACE AND MORAL RESPONSIBILITY

Because places matter to our health, our opportunities, and our experience of the world, as we saw in chapter 1, we have a moral responsibility to create good places for all. We may be uncomfortable with the claim that the location where one lives has such an influence on health, life expectancy, and educational and job opportunities, and yet we know it is true.

Places matter to God too. In the Old Testament, land was central to the Jewish ethical system. In this agrarian society, land represented economic opportunity. When the Hebrews entered the Promised Land, each tribe was given specific plots of land to ensure opportunity for everyone.

Old Testament land regulations protected the poor and dispossessed. Laws prevented owners from harvesting all the grain from their fields. Other laws gave the poor rights to glean in fields belonging to others. The tendency toward overexploitation was checked by the Sabbath Year, which required that the land be rested every seventh year. The tendency toward economic inequality was checked by the Year of Jubilee, which provided for a redistribution of land every fiftieth year (Lev. 25). Even if some became wealthy and others became poor, there was an opportunity every fifty years to rebalance the gains and losses. Future generations could look forward to renewed and equal opportunities.

We do not live in an agrarian society, however. Our places have changed in ways that challenge our ability to understand our moral obligations. In premodern times, places were often isolated and relatively self-sufficient. But in our contemporary world, places are interconnected with and depend on other places, near and far. Transportation and communication technologies have tied distant places together and created a truly global economy.

At the same time, our local places have thinned out. As the economy is increasingly globalized, we invest less in our local communities. We lose the depth of personal history, commitment, relatedness, and local control. We depend more on distant strangers to supply our food and other material needs. We interact less with those who live nearby. These changes challenge our ability to live ethically because they make it difficult for us to take moral account of the effects our life choices have on other people and places.

But we cannot shrink from this challenge. We began this book by thinking about our childhood homes. For most of us, a childhood home brings back memories of a house or perhaps a farm, street, or neighborhood. But as Christians, we are called to think more broadly about homes and places. We are called to do more than simply settle into a comfortable place for ourselves and our family. Loving our neighbors means ensuring they, too, live in good places. And our neighbors, as Jesus taught us, are not just our friends and acquaintances but all those who are made in God's image. Thus, we need to take moral responsibility not just for our own place but also for the other places to which it is connected.

Christians in North America have begun to think more carefully about God's call to care about their neighborhoods, cities, and regions. Christians have long operated ministries focused on the homeless and destitute population in cities, but various groups are now expanding their understanding of what it means to care. The ministries that are part of the Christian Community Development Association (CCDA) have broadened their gospel vision to include restoring the distressed neighborhoods where so many broken lives are found. Member organizations in the CCDA create jobs, build housing, and work for racial reconciliation. Another group, the Evangelical Environmental Network, has broadened the call for restoration to include animals, plants, and ecosystems. The Congress for the New Urbanism (CNU) is an international movement that works to design more attractive and livable neighborhoods. Within the CNU is a Christian caucus that connects the work of building more livable communities with Christian concerns for community, beauty, justice, and creation care.

The task of cultivating good places begins with where we live, work, and play. These places form the context for our actions. But our work of cultivation expands outward as we cross boundaries, cultivate shared spaces for a common life, and ensure that everyone has a place to call home. In the next chapter, we will explore some of these boundaries and how we might begin to cross them.

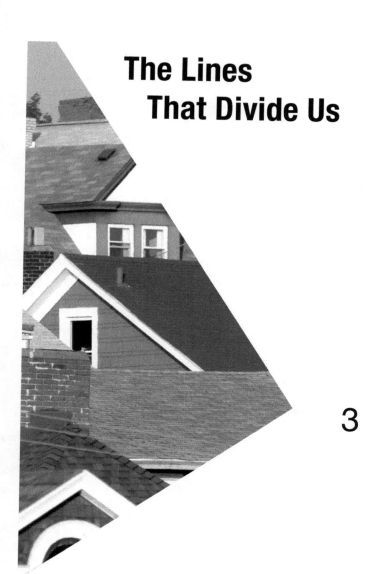

The Lines
That Divide Us

3

Before I built a wall I'd ask to know
What I was walling in or walling out,
And to whom I was like to give offence.
ROBERT FROST, "MENDING WALL"

DIVIDED LIVES

Residents of Flint, Michigan, had been drinking lead-tainted water for over a year when the story hit the national news in 2015. This city, where General Motors was founded and thrived for decades, has struggled since the 1980s with the loss of tens of thousands of automotive jobs and middle-class residents. Shuttered factories, empty stores, and vacant houses caused local tax revenues to plummet. Still, the streets needed to be plowed and patched. Pensions for retired city employees needed to be paid. Flint teetered on the edge of bankruptcy.

In 2011, the State of Michigan placed an emergency manager in charge of the city. Directed to balance the city's poor finances, the emergency manager decided to switch to a cheaper water source—the murky Flint River. The different chemistry of the turbid Flint River water leached lead from the city's aging pipes. The water at the tap was discolored and frequently unsafe to drink. Flint residents were exposed to dangerous levels of lead in their drinking water. Thousands of children, mostly African American, were exposed to a dangerous neurotoxin just because they had the misfortune to live in Flint.

But long before the public health problems in Flint were known, engineers at a local General Motors plant had their own suspicions about Flint's water supply. After the city switched to Flint River water, brand-new engine blocks started rusting on the factory floor. Luckily, the GM plant straddled the boundary between the city of Flint and the adjacent suburb of Flint Township. GM switched to Flint Township water. The problems stopped.

When the Flint water crisis hit the national news, the finger-pointing began. But what was forgotten in the blame game was that while Flint was nearly bankrupt, its suburbs were in much better financial shape. While Flint was making dangerous cost-cutting changes to its public water system, its suburbs were drinking the clean water that Flint could no longer afford. If the poor residents of Flint had been given the same option as the GM plant of switching to suburban water, they would have been fine. But Flint is a fragmented metropolitan region. Local municipal boundaries divide rich and poor, white and black. In Flint, city and suburb sometimes act like disconnected fiefdoms. And as if to prove the point, Flint Township is considering a name change to Carman Hills to avoid associations with the city of Flint.

Our world is a bordered world. The work of making places often begins with drawing borders. I live and work in the city of Grand Rapids, Michigan. But several blocks into my commute to work I am greeted by a welcome sign for the city of East Grand Rapids. Because I am a map geek, I know that I cross three more unmarked municipal boundaries on my three-mile commute, only to end up back in the city where I started. Just because municipal boundaries are often invisible doesn't mean they don't matter. These local boundaries determine where our kids go to school, how much we pay in property taxes, which politicians represent us, and what kind of city services we receive.

Creating borders is one way humans give order to God's world. The world maps hanging in our classrooms and church halls give prominent attention to the international borders between countries. In this chapter, we will explore the administrative boundaries between cities, counties, suburbs, townships, and school districts. These often-invisible lines divide us, sometimes even define us. Real estate agents know their importance. In many parts of the United States, the first question real estate agents ask their clients is which school district they want to live in. But most of us don't pay attention to the wider meaning of these dividing lines. We should because cultivating good places involves understanding and sometimes rethinking our local boundary lines.

CITY, SUBURB, OR METROPOLITAN REGION?

Ask someone where they live, and you will get a different answer depending on where you ask the question. Close to home, a person from the suburbs of Chicago will be sure to specify which suburb—Skokie, Wheaton, or Oak Park—they call home. If you happen to sit next to them on a flight from New York to London, they are more likely to answer, "Chicago" or "Chicagoland." The different answers stem from the fact that we live in politically fragmented metropolitan regions. You might ask, "What is a politically fragmented metropolitan region?" Let's find out.

A metropolitan region is an area of focused daily activity. A metropolitan region is larger than an individual city or suburb. It is the wider area within which we might search for a new job, a house, a used car, a plumber, or a church.

Here is one way to visualize your metropolitan region. Imagine a map showing all the places you and your family members spend your days. Your map should include your house, workplace, church, school, stores, gas stations, and parks. Geographers call that your daily activity space. Then imagine the daily activity space maps for all the people you regularly encounter. Visualize the daily lives of your garbage collector, work colleagues, and pastor. Your house might be in the Lincoln Park neighborhood of Chicago or on a hobby farm forty miles from the Chicago Loop. Your coworkers likely live in dozens of different neighborhoods and suburbs. The plumber who unplugged your sink may live in Cicero. Perhaps your landscapers live in Pilsen.

Combine all those daily activity space maps and you will have something close to a metropolitan region. In technical Census Bureau terms, the Chicagoland region is actually the Chicago-Naperville-Elgin metropolitan region. It is made up of fourteen counties and stretches across parts of three states.

In the course of our daily lives, we crisscross our metropolitan region. Often, we don't even notice when we cross from one suburb to another. But when it comes to choosing a house, then it suddenly matters which city, suburb, or township we call home. That is because our metropolitan regions are politically fragmented. Whether we live in Park Forest or Hinsdale makes a huge difference in the size of our property tax bill. When it comes to the quality of education, it matters whether our kids go to Cicero schools or Riverside schools.

Originally, the term *suburb* referred to a mostly residential neighborhood outside the city center. Over time, *suburb* came to mean a politically independent municipality. Each of these independent suburbs has its own laws and government. The Chicago metropolitan region has 1,550 units of local government. That makes the Chicago region an extreme example of metropolitan fragmentation.

CREATING DIVIDED REGIONS

How did we get our divided metropolitan regions? To answer that question, we must go back in time. America's largest cities grew large by regularly adjusting their borders outward as their populations grew. Cities gained territory by annexing small towns or undeveloped land. In 1889, Chicago annexed 133 square miles on its south side, bringing in Hyde Park and Pullman. When new neighborhoods developed beyond the city limits, they asked the city to adjust its borders. Growing neighborhoods wanted city services such as water, sewer, paved streets, and fire and police protection.

Annexation was usually a good deal for outlying settlements. Roxbury was once a rural area south of Boston with a sewage crisis. Roxbury residents begged to be annexed by Boston. Today, Roxbury is just another Boston neighborhood. Soon after Roxbury's annexation, the growing Brookline community faced a similar issue. Brookline, however, was home to many of the wealthiest Bostonians. Brookline rejected annexation in an 1873 vote. To this day, Brookline remains a politically independent city. Brookline's snub of Boston set the pattern for other affluent suburban communities. Like prodigal children, wealthy suburbs across the United States declared their political independence from the central cities that birthed them.

At the same time, state legislatures feared the growing power of corrupt big city governments. In response, many states passed laws making it more difficult for cities to annex new territory. Central cities lost the ability to regularly expand their borders. They were now landlocked. New growth spilled out beyond their borders. As streetcars and highways opened new land for development, more and more people chose to live in politically independent suburbs. The result was the politically fragmented metropolitan regions we have today.

Canadian provinces and some states, notably Arizona, North Carolina, and Texas, are more favorable to annexation. Thus, their central cities have been able to regularly expand their boundaries. But in the Northeast and Midwest, many central cities have not expanded their boundaries since the 1800s. These central cities are surrounded by scores or hundreds of newer politically independent communities.

The drawing of new municipal boundaries still goes on today. In the fast-growing Atlanta region, about a dozen new municipalities have been created in formerly unincorporated areas since 2005. Services once provided by the county are now provided by the newly created cities. Critics point out that the boundaries of these newly incorporated cities often divide white neighborhoods from black neighborhoods. The boundaries also seem to have been deliberately drawn to capture high-value properties and avoid low-value areas. Defenders argue that these new suburban cities give residents greater local control, lower taxes, and better public services.

Do the administrative boundaries that divide urban regions contribute to better places for all? Some scholars think metropolitan fragmentation is a good thing. But other scholars blame the fragmentation of local governments for all kinds of evils. We will examine the arguments in chapter 4.

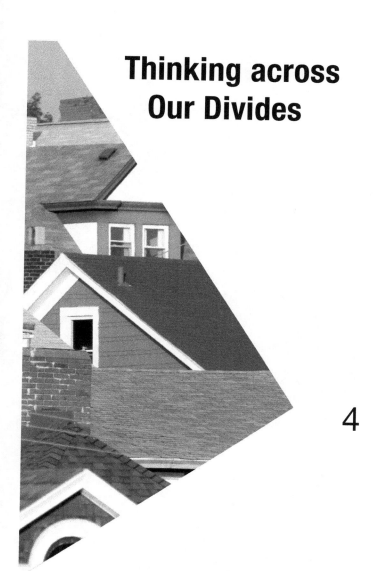

Thinking across
Our Divides

4

> Something there is that doesn't love a wall,
> That wants it down.
> ROBERT FROST, "MENDING WALL"

BORDERS CAN PROVIDE ORDER

Sometimes we need to draw borders. Imagine a moment of great unity sweeps across Chicagoland. All 1,550 local governments decide to merge. Hundreds and hundreds of mayors, school superintendents, and police chiefs all turn in their resignations. Then in an upset victory, you are elected mayor of this ten-million-person conglomerate. Think of the challenges you would face. Soon enough you would discover the difficulty in finding one-size-fits-all solutions to garbage, zoning, potholes, and education. Sometimes it makes sense to divide a metropolitan region into smaller parts. Borders can help provide order. Dividing up a territory can keep government local and closer to the people.

Part of the American democratic tradition is a preference for self-governance and limited government. It is easier to trust a government official you know personally. This is why when the newly acquired lands of the Louisiana Purchase were settled, the United States divided the land into townships. As Thomas Jefferson envisioned them, townships were to be small and self-governed. Several times per year residents would meet in the township hall to conduct their business. Township residents would decide how to maintain the local roads and ditches. Over time, urban growth reached these rural townships. Many once-rural townships incorporated and became independent suburbs. Looked at this way, our divided urban regions are simply an outgrowth of local democratic control.

Public choice theory argues that fragmented urban regions work better. The idea behind public choice theory is in its name. Economist Charles Tiebout, who popularized public choice theory, believed in choice and competition between cities. He favored metropolitan regions divided into numerous independent suburbs. That way people have more choices. Each city, township, and school district offers a different bundle of services at a particular tax rate. People examine their choices and choose the community that suits them best. People who want extravagant public services will pay higher property taxes. Those content with less can save on property taxes. On top of that, fragmentation encourages government efficiency, as cities and townships compete for residents.

Let's return to the example of my daily commute from chapter 3. When I pass through the suburb of East Grand Rapids on my way to work, I am greeted by a welcome sign with a picture of a sailboat. The sign also proclaims the city's motto, "A Better Place to Live." East Grand Rapids is a high-tax, high-service city. It has some of the highest-performing schools in Michigan. The parks are wonderful. The city provides free lawn waste cleanup. In winter, city crews plow the sidewalks in front of each house. And as expected, the city of East Grand Rapids has higher property tax rates than its neighbors.

Another line of support for fragmented metropolitan regions comes from the Roman Catholic principle of subsidiarity. Subsidiarity emphasizes that issues should be managed at the lowest level of authority capable of addressing an issue. Thus, the federal government should not take on issues better left to local school districts. We would not want the US Department of Education managing school transportation in Ottumwa, Iowa. On the other hand, we wouldn't want the Ottumwa city council making national defense policy. The essential insight of subsidiarity is that the *scale* of governance should match the *scale* of the issue being managed. Scale means the geographic extent—local, county, state, national, or international. There is obvious wisdom in the principle of subsidiarity, and as Americans, we like local democracy and choice. So what could be wrong with metropolitan fragmentation?

TROUBLING DIVIDES

There are both practical and theoretical arguments against metropolitan fragmentation. First, it is often inefficient. Many small units of government end up doing the same things. Economies of scale are lost. The greater efficiencies of larger units of government have driven a number of consolidations, such as the merger of Nashville and Davidson County.

A more theoretical argument against fragmentation goes back to the concept of subsidiarity. Essentially, governance should match the scale of an issue. However, too often the scale of our local governments fails to match the scale of our daily lives. Job and housing searches rarely stop at city borders. Yet individual cities and suburbs get to regulate where jobs and housing are located. An independent suburb might be able to run its own parks and school system, but it can't build a regional highway system, trail network, or public transit system. It probably wouldn't be able to provide its own water and sewerage systems.

One of the key lessons of ecology is that everything is connected. Upstream actions affect those living downstream. Rivers, aquifers, and air pollution don't stop at municipal boundaries. Solving environmental problems requires cooperation across municipal lines. The affluent city of East Grand Rapids three times voted down proposals to merge with Grand Rapids. But when it suffered a severe drinking water and sewage crisis, it found that the only solution was to connect to Grand Rapids's water and sewer.

The natural world also suffers from fragmentation. Parks provide better ecological habitat when they connect to other parks. Divided urban regions lack interconnected park systems. Lacking ecological corridors, birds and mammals are isolated and unable to migrate. In short, fragmentation leaves a gap when it comes to managing regional systems and fixing regional problems.

Fragmentation also halts the natural growth of the core city. Cities that are surrounded by independent suburbs are landlocked. They cannot capture their own outward expansion. New residents, new housing subdivisions, new shopping centers, and new office parks do not contribute to the core city. Instead, new growth competes with the old core city. Such cities are called under-bounded. Under-bounded cities often experience a spiral of decline and fiscal squeeze. They have the oldest buildings and the oldest infrastructure. Thus, they attract the region's poorest residents. Middle-class residents and their pocketbooks depart for the suburbs, reducing leadership and tax revenues.

Under-bounded cities tend to decline in population. Cities with flexible boundaries tend to grow. The boundaries of Saint Louis, Missouri, have not changed since 1876. This under-bounded city lost 64 percent of its population between 1950 and 2017. Saint Louis residents have median household incomes only two-thirds those of the entire region. The under-bounded city provides life and services to its growing suburbs, but it receives little in return.

The welcome sign for East Grand Rapids suggests another problem with fragmentation: inequality. The city's tagline "A Better Place to Live" raises the question "Better than what?" The implied comparison with Grand Rapids suggests competition and choice. But it also suggests there are winners and losers. Fragmentation is troubling when the region's lawyers, doctors, and managers live in one municipality and their housecleaners and lawn service workers live in another.

A TALE OF TWO CITIES

In public choice theory, people sort themselves into different municipalities and school districts based on their preferences for services and their willingness to pay taxes. But imagine a metropolitan region made up of just two equal-sized cities. The first city has the more expensive housing and is home to the business owners and professionals. The second city has more modest housing and is home to the low-wage workers. Over time, office parks and shopping centers relocate closer to their clientele in the rich city. The rich city has higher property values, so it can fund high-quality schools, parks, and services while keeping tax rates low.

Meanwhile, as the poorer city loses businesses, its tax revenues decline. It is forced to raise tax rates to cover the basics. Higher taxes speed the departure of the residents and businesses that can afford to leave. Faced with a shrinking population of low-income residents and low-value housing, the poor city offers poor-quality services at high tax rates. The poor city spirals downward, along with its trapped residents.

Local governments can speed up the sorting of rich and poor through their controls over land. To improve their bottom line, they can zone land to maximize revenues and minimize expenses. This is called fiscal zoning. The specifics vary from state to state, but in general, the optimal fiscal zoning allows only high-priced housing and commercial buildings. A key part of fiscal zoning is to keep out low-income housing, which brings large numbers of children to educate.

In our hypothetical example, the richer city adopts fiscal zoning practices. It requires large lots for houses and forbids apartments. These rules drive up housing prices. Only those families who are better off can choose the richer city. Thus, fiscal zoning filters out the poor.

COULD THIS REALLY HAPPEN?

The above scenario may sound too bleak to be true. But study after study of fragmented metropolitan regions shows it is happening. Some state governments assist cities to help even out local budgets. Michigan tends to leave local governments on their own. And in the early 2000s, eighteen local governments in Michigan—twelve cities, one county, and five school districts—entered financial emergency status as they teetered on the edge of bankruptcy. In each case, the suffering communities were bordered by more affluent communities in good fiscal shape. The impacts of Michigan's local fiscal crises fell unevenly. During Detroit's bankruptcy, the cities controlled by emergency financial managers housed half the state's African American population.

Detroit illustrates the problems of metropolitan fragmentation. When Detroit declared bankruptcy in 2013, it was the largest municipal bankruptcy in US history. Yet in the early and middle decades of the twentieth century, Detroit was a beacon of prosperity. Until the early 1960s, Detroit relied on property taxes for its revenues. Then, facing the loss of residents and businesses to its suburbs, it gained permission from the state legislature to impose a 1 percent income tax on workers and/or residents of the city. That immediately boosted the city's finances.

However, in the late 1960s, the city experienced race riots, white flight, and the relocation of industry to the suburbs. The city doubled the local income tax rate in 1969, raised property taxes by 30 percent in 1974, and increased the local income tax to 3 percent in 1982. The city added utility taxes and casino wagering taxes. Each new tax increased revenues and encouraged residents and businesses to leave. In a fragmented region, people quickly realized that they could escape Detroit's taxes by moving across the city line.

The population of Detroit dropped from a peak of 1.85 million in 1950 to under 700,000 today. At the time of its bankruptcy, Detroit had the highest local income taxes and the highest property tax rates in Michigan. And what did Detroit residents get for those high tax rates? Not much. An estimated 40 percent of the streetlights did not work. Roads were in terrible shape. Police and fire response times were unacceptable. The school system faced massive challenges.

Detroit's bankruptcy was inevitable because individual and public choices had concentrated poverty and resources on opposite sides of political boundaries. While Detroit had $9,400 of taxable property per person, the nearby suburb of Grosse Pointe Farms had $78,300. The border between Detroit and its Grosse Pointe suburbs marks a stark geographic divide. On one side, houses are in various states of decay—boarded up, burned, collapsing, or overgrown with vegetation. On the other side is a landscape of stylish houses and manicured lawns. On the Detroit side, residents struggle against poverty, dysfunctional schools, and crime. Life in Grosse Pointe centers on school musicals, garden parties, tennis lessons, country clubs, and Caribbean vacations.

The neighborhoods on the Detroit side of the border range from 75 to 98 percent African American. Meanwhile, of the thirteen census tracts in Grosse Pointe, four do not house a single African American. Most are below 1 percent African American. It is true that you don't need a passport to cross the Detroit–Grosse Pointe border. However, to use the "public" parks in Grosse Pointe, you do need a city-issued, residents-only park pass with photo identification.

Another problem with fragmentation is that it undermines cooperation for the common good. Oakland County is a prosperous suburban county across the infamous Eight Mile Road from the city of Detroit. For many decades, the trademark of some Oakland County politicians was to oppose everything Detroit wanted. If Detroit wanted transit improvements, these politicians would fight it. Thus, metropolitan Detroit still lacks a regional public transit system that serves both city and suburbs.

THE CHILDREN OF DIVIDED REGIONS

A final argument against metropolitan fragmentation focuses on opportunities for young people. In biblical times, economic opportunity was tied to the land. In the Old Testament, the allocation of land among the Hebrew tribes created a level playing field. Gleaning laws and the Year of Jubilee created opportunities for those left behind. In today's information society, education is the key to economic opportunity. Thus, middle- and upper-income parents work vigorously to give their children the best possible education. They seek out the highest-rated school districts. The best schools, not surprisingly, are usually found in areas with the most expensive housing. Thus, a child's life chances are tied to their family's economic status.

How much children learn in school depends a great deal on the other children in the classroom. Dense concentrations of poverty can harm learning. Negative peer influences, lowered expectations, frequent moves, and a lack of resources undermine success. Fragmentation plays a role because it leads to greater segregation in schools. And since education influences future life chances, metropolitan fragmentation perpetuates inequality. Too often a child's economic status determines their postal code. And in a divided region, one's postal code can determine one's chances in life.

CROSSING DIVIDING LINES

We inherit our political boundaries from past generations. But borders are what we make of them. The political fragmentation of urban regions is an entrenched reality in the United States. It gives some people choice and local control. But when local administrative boundaries are drawn along lines of income and race, it can be disastrous. Fragmentation can deepen inequality and strengthen fear and suspicion. Many boundaries were created and many borders are still maintained by processes that are saturated with conflict between those who have much and those who have less. Indeed, the history of political fragmentation reminds us that it benefits the wealthiest members of society. It allows them to secede from the rest of the region and hoard their resources.

As Christians, we can accept the legitimacy of local control in the name of subsidiarity. We might want to rephrase the preference for local control as getting the scale of governance right. We can endorse a preference for smaller government where it is appropriate. But we must question the unwillingness of privileged places to open their borders and share their resources. Good places need boundaries, but not boundaries that divide haves from have-nots. Good places need dividing lines that are porous and do not isolate the poor. And good places need shared spaces where we can build community, the topic of chapter 5.

The Spaces
We Share

5

> The street, the square, the park, the market, the
> playground are the river of life.
>
> KATHLEEN MADDEN, PROJECT FOR PUBLIC SPACES

PUBLIC SPACES AND PUBLIC LIFE

My wife grew up in Minneapolis near Lake Harriet. Almost every day she walked her golden retriever on the three-mile path around the lake. In summer, she swam at one of the four public beaches on the lake. On warm nights, her family biked to free concerts at the band shelter on the opposite shore. The nightly concerts drew as broad a cross section of urban and suburban dwellers as one could imagine. She relished the people watching—walkers, joggers, bikers, skaters, and concertgoers of all sizes, colors, and ages.

When we moved to Grand Rapids, Michigan, we chose a house near Reeds Lake, an urban lake that resembled Lake Harriet. Soon, however, we noticed some big differences. There is no continuous public path around Reeds Lake. Nearly all of the shoreline of Reeds Lake is privately owned. There are no public beaches. There are only private beaches restricted to members of the yacht club or private lake associations. Reeds Lake, with its private control over the best parts of the landscape, is actually the more common scenario in North America. Minneapolis, the "City of Lakes," is quite unusual in the abundance of its public park space. Back in the 1880s, its citizens voted to buy all the undeveloped waterfront in the city to create a vast park system for everyone to enjoy. The abundance of public spaces in Minneapolis and their relative absence in Grand Rapids give the two cities a strikingly different feel.

Created in the image of the Triune God who is a community of love, we were made for relationships. As T. S. Eliot asked, "What life is there that is not lived in community?" The public spaces of a community create a framework for the shared life of a people. Public spaces are those facilities and pieces of land that are open for anyone to use. Typically, they are publicly owned and include parks, plazas, playgrounds, libraries, and community gardens. Public spaces also include the land set aside as right-of-way for streets, highways, sidewalks, and trails. Good places need good public spaces so people can travel freely, congregate, socialize, and engage in recreational and cultural activities. Parks support community life and the enjoyment of God's creation. Sidewalks, streets, and public transportation systems open up a city to everyone by linking public and private spaces together.

No person is an island, self-sufficient for sustenance and well-being. Everyone relies on public spaces in their everyday life. Public spaces are the setting for the unfolding of communal life: the movement of goods and people and festal gatherings. But for the poor and most vulnerable, public spaces are especially important. A city's parks are the poor person's living room.

A healthy life involves a balance between the intimacy and security of the private home and the openness of the public sphere. Different cultures draw the lines between public and private in different ways. But in the late twentieth century, the balance in North America tilted toward the private refuge. A host of changes to urban life undermined the public realm. Now is the time to find new ways to live in community in today's cities and suburbs. This chapter explores the shared spaces that are essential to community life and the challenges they face.

PUBLIC SPACES AND THE CHRISTIAN LIFE

In John's description of the New Jerusalem in Revelation 22, God dwells with his people in a garden city. In the center of the city, emanating from God's throne, is a broad plaza. The river of the water of life flows down the center of the plaza. Along each bank of the river, the tree of life grows. Here is a vision of the truly good place: public space, water, trees, worshipers from all nations, and the presence of the living God.

Not surprisingly, then, a consistent feature of places built by Christian communities has been the centrality of public spaces. The medieval European town, despite its imperfections, was designed for the collective living of the Christian life. Medieval towns featured cramped dwellings on narrow streets. Making up for the lack of private space was a spacious central plaza that served as the center of civic, social, and religious life. Bordered by the cathedral and city hall, plazas were filled with activity—markets, church processions, holiday festivities, weddings, and other communal events. Whether called a plaza, piazza, platz, place, or plein, the central public space remains the primary gathering place in European towns and cities.

During the Spanish colonization of the New World, the Law of the Indies stipulated that towns be built with a central plaza. Today, central plazas remain the defining feature of Latin American cities. The Puritans also built their New England villages with a broad vision of communal life. Their settlements featured a central village green bordered by a meetinghouse. The village green was used for grazing livestock, relaxation, civic gatherings, and church picnics. Today, the Boston Common and the New Haven Green are living legacies of seventeenth-century Puritan city planning. These parks at the heart of modern cities provide space for civic functions and a green respite from urban clamor.

Sadly, the great models for public space found in medieval European, Spanish colonial, and Puritan towns were often forgotten. Most North American cities were shaped more by the profit motive than by theology. The most valuable, central land went to the highest bidder. Usually, that happened to be the office tower, department store, railroad terminal, or factory. A brief nineteenth-century urban parks movement tried to counter this trend. Advocates thought parks could improve public health and promote social harmony. This parks movement produced many of North America's most popular public spaces. Examples include New York's Central Park, Boston's Emerald Necklace, Chicago's Lakefront, and Minneapolis's Grand Rounds Parkways.

Our newest cities and suburbs often lack the great public spaces that we love in older cities. In the second half of the twentieth century, city building took new directions. City builders produced opulent private spaces at the expense of the shared realm. Multifunctional public spaces were replaced with spaces serving a single function such as shopping or driving. To cultivate good places, we must understand the changes that have transformed the physical and social fabric of our communities.

MACHINE SPACES

The street right-of-way is probably the most important public space in our communities. In boomtowns or haphazardly planned towns, the street right-of-way is the only public space. Historically, the public street was a combination of passageway, civic arena, and gathering space. Prior to the rise of the automobile, public streets were a riot of activity. Streets were the domain of commerce, transportation, and social life. Streets were home to pedestrians, horse-drawn wagons and carriages, watering troughs, playing children, vendors, beggars, political rallies, and wandering fowl and livestock. In the late nineteenth century, bicycles, streetcars, and automobiles joined the frenzied mix.

With great difficulty and numerous tragic mishaps, the automobile emerged on top. Other street users had to be banished so automobiles could move swiftly and unimpeded to their destinations. Streets were redefined as the domain of automobiles. The once multifunctional public space of the street came to serve a single function: the swift conveyance of motorized traffic. Streets were redesigned to meet the needs of fast-moving vehicles. Roads were paved and widened. Speed limits increased. Crossing the street became dangerous for pedestrians.

The US Interstate Highway System took the logic further. It is the greatest engineering work in human history. It is also the epitome of a single-function public space. Its design priorities are speed and traffic capacity. Pedestrians, bicycles, and slow-moving vehicles are not allowed.

The speed and effortless movement of automobile travel allowed cities to sprawl outward. Over time, the spread-out developments built for the automobile became impossible to access except by automobile. As automobile ownership expanded, walking came to be seen as obsolete. Walking was redefined as a leisure activity, not a means to actually get somewhere. City planners didn't bother to require sidewalks, and developers were glad to save the expense. The street right-of-way came to be dominated by a single user: motorized vehicles.

There is a great inefficiency in the use of private automobiles. The size of the vehicle dwarfs that of its passengers. Vast areas of our communities must be paved over and dedicated to storing automobiles. Every business is required by zoning laws to have enough parking to handle the busiest imaginable day. So most of the time, most parking spots go unused. Churches are among the worst offenders. Their parking lots are used for just a few hours on Sunday mornings.

Study a Google Earth satellite image of your city's business districts. Look at the amount of land dedicated to moving and storing cars and trucks. Geographers call this machine space. In some business districts, machine space covers more than two-thirds of the land area. Scant leftover space remains for buildings, bicycles, pedestrians, and green space.

PUBLIC TRANSIT

Public transit shaped the cities we have inherited from the past. Until they went into decline in the 1950s, streetcars were a shared space used by people from all walks of life. Streetcars transported users, rich and poor alike, almost anywhere they wanted to go. But as cars grew in popularity, conflict was inevitable. Streetcar tracks took up valuable road space. Which mode of transportation would dominate the streets? The private automobile won. With the exception of a handful of large cities with good commuter rail, subway, or light rail systems, public transit has become the domain of the poor, the disabled, and those too young or too old to drive.

When designers and builders focus on the needs of automobiles, public transit suffers. Automobiles promise freedom and often deliver. But as we rearranged our cities to meet the needs of our cars, we became enslaved in a state of automobile dependency. Public transit systems have a very difficult time serving sprawling, automobile-based destinations. Thus, people without access to an automobile find many work and shopping opportunities off-limits.

Further, something was lost when we built our way of life around the automobile. The once-common experience of sharing space through public transportation is increasingly rare. Even though two city bus lines stop outside my place of employment, they are *terra incognita* for most of my students and colleagues. In my hometown of Grand Rapids, Michigan, most of the major corporate employers are in suburbs not reachable by transit. When I board the city bus, I enter a different city—one that is mostly African American and Latino. On the city bus, I share space and rub shoulders with people from different walks of life. On the city bus, I learn to wait for my fellow citizens who move a little slower or have disabilities. I sometimes find myself resenting the extra time to load and secure a wheelchair on board the bus. But then I remember that my dad spent the last fifteen years of his life confined to a wheelchair and mostly trapped at home.

Machine spaces are neither pleasant nor safe for transit users or pedestrians. Picture the area around your nearest shopping mall or big box retail center. How friendly and welcoming is that space to transit users? How far is it from the bus stop to the door of the mall? How pleasant would it be to cross that distance in winter or summer? Are there protected shelters, sidewalks, and safe street crossings?

The tragic death of Buffalo, New York, teenager Cynthia Nicole Wiggins is a reminder of the dangers of machine spaces. Wiggins was killed by a dump truck while trying to cross seven lanes of traffic. Wiggins, who was African American, had ridden the bus from her home in a poor, inner-city neighborhood. She was hit while walking from the bus stop to the Walden Galleria shopping mall, where she worked. The mall owners had rejected requests to install a bus stop on mall property, fearing it would attract the wrong type of customer. So instead the bus stop was located across a busy road from the mall where there were no sidewalks, crosswalks, or pedestrian signals. The cost of this decision was the life of a young woman.

SHOPPING MALLS AS TOWN CENTERS

When the automobile took over in the second half of the twentieth century, places built for walking or public transit went into decline. Shopping shifted to shopping centers and enclosed shopping malls. Older places could not compete with the mall's free parking, controlled environment, and unlimited selection of goods. Traditional retail streets lost customers. Downtown department stores closed. Small-town Main Streets were left with vacant storefronts.

Ironically, shopping mall storefronts often mimicked the Main Street facades they replaced. Mall food courts tried to emulate the historic town squares they undermined. In recent decades, enclosed shopping malls have started to lose their luster. Online shopping has eaten into their profits. Some malls have shed their roofs and become open-air lifestyle centers. Lifestyle centers look and feel even more like old-fashioned town centers or Main Streets.

While some are nostalgic for the past, suburban malls and lifestyle centers are convenient and efficient places to shop. They can be a pleasant substitute for the loss of town centers and Main Streets. But beneath their surface, something is quite different. Main Streets and city sidewalks are publicly owned. Today's shopping complexes have a single owner, and their "public" spaces are actually privately controlled.

Town centers attract a diverse mixture of uses and users. Downtowns have office buildings, apartments, concert halls, churches, stores, government buildings, and more. City sidewalks offer a variety of random social encounters. You might encounter someone collecting signatures for a political referendum or a person begging for spare change. By comparison, the private shopping complex offers a narrower range of activities and a more predictable experience. After all, malls and lifestyle centers are managed and operated for one primary purpose: profits. They are palaces of consumption.

My extended family lives in Minneapolis, where the rotunda of the Mall of America has become the primary venue for large community events. During holidays, there are organized festivities and school choir concerts. In between, there are new product launches, book signings, theatrical auditions, sports rallies, and celebrity visits. However, certain public activities are not allowed in this privately owned and controlled space. Activities that undermine the mall's primary function of shopping are unwelcome. Distributing religious or political fliers, circulating a petition, or panhandling will earn you a swift escort to an exit.

Courts have ruled that rights of assembly and free speech that we have in public spaces do not apply in a privately controlled space like a shopping mall. Anti-fur and Black Lives Matter protesters have lost court cases over their right to hold protests at the Mall of America. The courts' decisions mean that our new town centers do not have to allow political speech. Malls may look like public spaces, but they are not.

HARDENED PUBLIC SPACES

Just when older downtowns were struggling with the loss of shoppers to suburban malls, the country's homeless population began to soar. The causes were complex.

There was the closing of state psychiatric institutions, rising chemical addiction, family breakdown, and the loss of affordable housing. Homeless persons, with no place to retreat to, were forced to use whatever public spaces were available. Thus, they congregated in the remaining public spaces of the city. Public squares became zones of conflict between latte-sipping office workers, museum-going families, panhandlers, and homeless persons trying to catch some sleep.

In places where the homeless gathered, many cities hardened the space to make them feel unwelcome. Public bathrooms disappeared. Jagged steel ridges were installed on walls and ledges to prevent sitting. Armrests were added to park benches to prevent sleeping. New laws and regulations restricted the use of public spaces. In many cities, it became illegal to beg, lie down, or sleep in public places. The result was a more hostile, less welcoming public space for everyone.

TIME TRAVELERS PAY A VISIT

Time travelers from the 1890s or 1950s would be in for quite a shock upon visiting our contemporary cities. They would be awed by our spacious suburban houses and high-speed expressways. But they would also notice that something tragic has happened. Walking and transit options are nonexistent in many places. More importantly, we lack the shared spaces that support a common life. The loss of public spaces is partly the result of new technologies and partly the product of human desires for comfort and convenience. It is also a result of social breakdown and a growing fear of strangers.

The automobile, highway, shopping mall, and online shopping, however, are here to stay. So what solutions are available? One response to our time travelers' complaints would be to take them on a tour of a new master-planned neighborhood. In a master-planned neighborhood, there are abundant shared spaces—trails, parks, pools, and playgrounds for building a common life. Some master-planned neighborhoods, especially those influenced by the New Urbanism, even imitate old town centers. In chapter 6, we will explore such neighborhoods as a possible solution to our need for shared spaces.

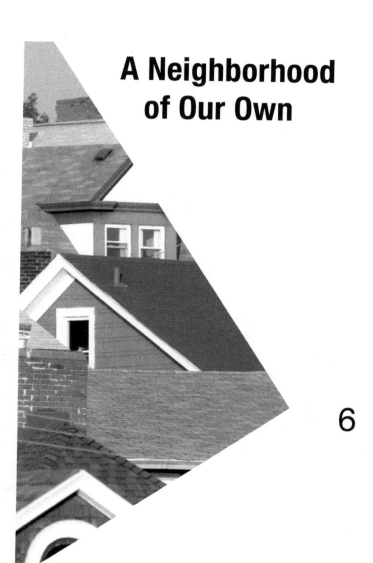

A Neighborhood
of Our Own

6

> The house itself is of minor importance. Its relation
> to the community is the thing that really counts.
>
> CLARENCE STEIN

NEIGHBORHOOD SPACES

I had grown excited reading about a new type of neighborhood called the New Urbanism. So I was thrilled to visit the first New Urbanist development to be built near Minneapolis. With a car full of geography students, I headed to Liberty on the Lake. Just as we pulled in, the skies cleared after a June thunderstorm. Everything was fresh and sparkling in the sunlight. All seemed perfect. Each house featured a front porch and a pair of rocking chairs. In the center of the neighborhood was a town square with an elegant pavilion. And as if to confirm our first impressions, we spotted the following scene: A group of boys on bikes stopped at the edge of the street. They stooped over and scooped water into their hands. Then, as if they were standing in a mountain stream, they drank deeply from the rivulet flowing down the gutter.

The New Urbanism is a response to the loss of public spaces described in chapter 5. The New Urbanism offer strategies for walkable neighborhoods, public spaces that foster social interaction, and Main Streets and city centers that are full of life. But the New Urbanism is just the latest in a long history of attempts to build better neighborhoods. Let's explore these attempts to create good neighborhoods for everyone.

FROM UTOPIA TO SUBURBIA

Thomas More's *Utopia* inspired the creation of ideal towns in Europe and the Americas. It even influenced planned suburban communities. From the 1600s through the mid-1900s, ideal towns always featured generous public spaces. In the 1700s and 1800s, communal Christian groups built utopian towns with names like Bethlehem and Harmony. In the early and mid-1900s, garden cities and New Towns blended the best of town and country with an inclusive social vision. In recent decades, utopian town planning crystallized into a new form: the master-planned private neighborhood. Earlier utopian ideals of social equality, religious devotion, or collective ownership of fields and factories fell by the wayside. What survived was an emphasis on aesthetics and shared community facilities.

MASTER-PLANNED NEIGHBORHOODS

After World War II, subdivisions grew larger. Mass production methods were applied to housing. The Levitt Brothers built entire cities in what were farm fields outside

Philadelphia and New York City. Levittown, near Phila-delphia, encompassed twenty-two square miles and more than 17,300 houses. The original Levittown used just six house models. The near-identical houses lent uniformity to the community.

In the 1920s, a few builders had started thinking beyond the individual house. They master planned entire neighborhoods, giving them distinct identities. In the 1960s, visionary developers tried to improve on cook-ie-cutter subdivisions of identical houses. Robert Simon planned and built the sixty-thousand-person New Town of Reston, Virginia, in suburban Washington, DC. His vision was to create a strong community through shared spaces. In Reston, each house was to be within walking distance of a communal tennis court and swimming pool. Reston's neighborhoods were linked together with walk-ing trails winding through preserved woodlands.

Master-planned private neighborhoods are now the norm in many regions of North America. Builders can charge higher prices when they design an entire com-munity as a package experience. They impart exclusivity through curving streets, architectural styles, and pres-tigious names. Take, for example, Manchester Hills in suburban Grand Rapids. The entrances to the neighbor-hood feature stone walls, wrought iron fencing, mock guard towers, and fountains. The houses in Manchester Hills all look like storybook castles and are set on winding streets with names like Nottinghill Court.

Amenities are an essential part of planned neighborhoods. Pools, tennis courts, playgrounds, trails, and clubhouses are typical. To ensure their ongoing maintenance, developers set up a system of common ownership and private governance. In condominiums, an association owns and manages the shared hallways and party rooms. Similarly, in a private, master-planned neighborhood, there are homeowner associations (HOAs). HOAs collect mandatory dues for maintenance of the shared facilities. HOAs are essentially private governments. But HOAs differ from normal governments. Local government charters address goals such as promoting the welfare of all people. The charters of HOAs, on the other hand, focus on property values.

Houses in neighborhoods with HOAs make up about half of all new housing in the larger urban areas of the United States. They are certainly here to stay. They offer residents a comfortable retreat from the problems of urban life. Here residents find compensation for the loss of shared spaces in the city. The rise of master-planned communities shows the importance of shared spaces. We are social beings, and we like to identify with a community and know our neighbors. The shared spaces of the private, master-planned neighborhood create opportunities for social interaction. Plus, there is not enough lakeshore or beach for everyone to have their own private piece of it. It is inefficient for every house to have its own swimming pool and tennis court. By pooling resources, we can all have a better place to live.

If people want to pay extra to live in a master-planned neighborhood with extra amenities, what is the problem? Well, it turns out that private neighborhoods have public effects. The communal spaces of private neighborhoods are a far cry from the New England village green or a city park. Private neighborhoods create a strong sense of "us" and "them." Master-planned neighborhoods provide a more luxurious commons for their residents. But it comes at the expense of narrowing the definition of "public" to just owners and their guests. Most private neighborhoods have a limited range of house prices, and some have age restrictions. This means that residents share their common spaces with people a lot like themselves.

The guard towers at the Manchester Hills neighborhood are just for looks. But many master-planned neighborhoods include perimeter walls and gates controlled by security guards or access cards. Across the United States, about 15 percent of all houses in subdivisions are in gated or walled communities. That number rises in the Sun Belt and reaches 50 percent in the Los Angeles region. Gates and walls send the message that only certain people belong. On a practical level, gated neighborhoods reduce the amount of the city available to dog walkers, runners, and Girl Scouts selling cookies.

Before we embrace the private, master-planned neighborhood as a solution to the loss of public spaces, we need to consider its relationships with those outside its boundaries. Will residents identify more with their private neighborhood or with the wider city? Will those who reside in private neighborhoods be willing to pay taxes to support public parks, public beaches, lifeguards, and trails that duplicate what they already have? As the successful secede into master-planned private neighborhoods, will they lose social connections with their fellow citizens? Will our common life suffer?

NEW URBANIST SOLUTIONS?

The New Urbanist movement recognizes that something is wrong with the way we build communities. The New Urbanists mourn the decline of our city centers and Main Streets. They bemoan the fact that our streets have become machine spaces rather than places for all types of users. They cringe at our shopping districts dominated by parking lots and our residential streets lined with faceless garage doors. They worry that children can't walk to school or the corner store. They fear that neighbors don't know one another.

The solution, according to the New Urbanists, is better design. New Urbanists call for houses set close together, front porches, sidewalks, town squares, and mixed-use buildings with shops on the first floor and apartments above. They have succeeded in producing some beautiful neighborhoods, such as Seaside, Florida, and Kentlands in Gaithersburg, Maryland. They have even influenced the US Department of Housing and Urban Development's reconstruction of scores of public housing projects. Without exception, New Urbanist communities feature wonderful shared spaces. At their best, New Urbanist communities are integrated into existing neighborhoods, offer housing for a wide range of people, and have public spaces open to all.

The New Urbanism makes a good start in reclaiming the public realm for a common life. But it hasn't gone far enough. Too often New Urbanism has not countered the privatism at work in master-planned communities. Many of the leading New Urbanist communities are exclusive resorts or high-end suburbs. The parks, playgrounds, pavilions, and trails in some New Urbanist communities display "Residents Only" signs. Some New Urbanist communities are gated.

Another shortcoming of the New Urbanism is its failure to ensure good neighborhoods for all. The New Urbanism calls for a diversity of housing types and residents. But too often it is reduced to an aesthetic style. When built by for-profit developers, New Urbanist neighborhoods tend to focus on the upper end of the housing market. Thus, the New Urbanist movement needs to broaden its vision to include providing good housing for all, the subject of the next two chapters.

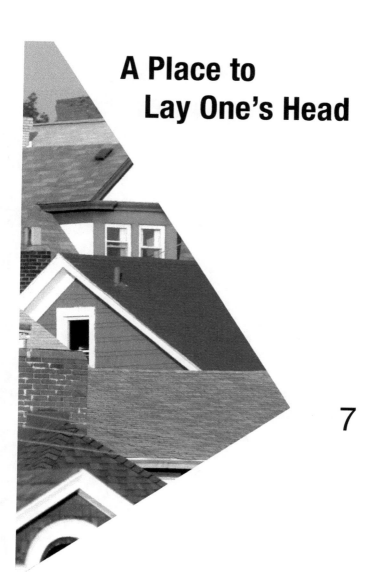

A Place to Lay One's Head

7

My people will live in peaceful dwelling places,
in secure homes,
in undisturbed places of rest.

Isaiah 32:18

HOUSING AND HUMAN NEEDS

We humans need shelter. Have you ever spent a night without a proper shelter? Was it miserable? For me, there was the camping trip when my friend Dan accidentally packed a picnic tablecloth instead of a tent. Much worse, a former roommate spent an entire winter sleeping in his car in Minneapolis after getting out of the Navy. Such experiences drive home the value of having a good place to lay one's head. Yet houses are more than mere shelter. They are usually the places where we feel most at home. They are where we feel warmth, belonging, security, and a sense of control.

Psychologist Abraham Maslow developed a theory of human needs, depicting them stacked on top of each other like the layers of a pyramid. At the base of the pyramid are bodily needs. These must be met first before building upward. Needs for safety, belonging, self-esteem, and self-actualization complete the pyramid. Houses meet human needs at each level in Maslow's hierarchy.

At the base of the pyramid, a house provides shelter from the elements. Next, a house offers a place of security for our bodies and our most treasured possessions. Picture a homeless person with all their worldly belongings piled into a shopping cart. Third, a house offers a setting for relationships. Houses are where our families grow and build memories. A house gives us an address. It places us within a community and gives us neighbors to love. Moving up the hierarchy, a house contributes to self-esteem. For rich and poor alike, one's house is a source of pride and a marker of achievement. Finally, atop Maslow's hierarchy, a house becomes a means of self-expression. Architecture, gardening, and interior decorations express who we are.

Everyone seems obsessed with houses these days. Economists eagerly await the release of the latest house construction numbers. Magazines and entire television networks are dedicated to house hunting, house make-overs, and house flipping. Stars of home renovation television programs are top celebrities. Compared to people in other countries, most North Americans are luxuriously housed.

At the same time, there are signs of trouble in our housing systems. High housing costs in many cities leave households struggling with affordability. In Vancouver, BC, the average house costs thirteen times the median annual income (a ratio of 3.0 or lower is considered affordable). When real estate markets are hot, homeowners become wealthy while renters suffer. The house fever that makes some rich locks others out of homeownership. Many pay too much in rent. Still others are homeless. If the homeless population of the United States were a city, it would be ranked the thirty-third largest in the country.

Since houses meet so many human needs, they deserve careful consideration. In this chapter, we will explore how housing systems work.

ODDITIES OF HOUSING MARKETS

Few of us build our own houses. So to understand housing, we must know something about construction, financing, real estate sales, and government regulations. The vast majority of housing in North America is furnished by the private market system. Government plays important roles, but not so much in the sense of actually building houses. In fact, the percentage of housing built and owned by the government—public housing—is tiny and shrinking.

While houses meet many human needs, they are also commodities. We buy and sell them like cars and dishwashers. The desire for profit motivates real estate developers, lenders, sales agents, buyers, and investors. When real estate is hot, ordinary families will flip houses as a second income. A recent count yielded 328 books for sale on Amazon instructing readers how to get rich flipping houses. The fever for speculative real estate profits can get out of control. House flipping pushes prices higher and higher and was a major cause of the housing price bubble that caused the Great Recession of 2007–2009.

Our houses are the places where our dreams and financial schemes intersect. Most visions of the American Dream involve a detached, single-family house, perhaps with a three-car garage and a white picket fence. About two-thirds of US households own their own house, and more would if they could. But houses are fundamentally different from other consumer goods. Houses are very expensive, long lasting, and pretty much fixed in place. Investing in a house offers advantages compared to investments in stocks, bonds, or mutual funds. When you buy a house, you get tax advantages, and you get to use and benefit from that asset for as long as you own it. For most families, their house is their largest store of wealth. However, much of the value of a house depends on its surroundings and other factors outside the owner's control.

A real estate dictum states that the value of a house depends on three factors: location, location, and location. Location matters in multiple ways. First, the strength of the regional economy matters. That is why houses are so cheap in Detroit and the rural Midwest. A three-bedroom ranch house in San Jose, California, would sell for the same price as ten to twenty identical houses in small towns across the Midwest. But the regional scale is not one over which most homeowners have much choice or influence. We live in particular regions because that is where our roots, our families, and/or our jobs are located. Second, inside a region, particular suburbs and school districts are more desirable and command higher prices. Closer to home, one's immediate surroundings make a difference. Smelly factories and boarded-up houses reduce nearby property values. On the other hand, a new park nearby will raise property values. In short, real estate is subject to spillover effects.

So as homebuyers prepare to invest much of their wealth in a durable, nonmovable asset whose value depends on its surroundings, how do they respond? They seek security for their housing investment. As their finances allow, they choose the best school districts and the best municipalities. They try to predict the geographic patterns of neighborhood decline and price appreciation. They move out when signs of decline appear. They are told to buy the cheapest house in the best neighborhood they can afford. That way, the values of their neighbors' houses pull theirs upward. And they try to influence city zoning and planning rules to enhance the value of their own property. If an affordable housing complex is proposed for their neighborhood, they might protest the increased traffic. If their neighborhood becomes hot and is in demand for new condominiums and apartments, they might protest the increased density. And if their protests are successful in stopping new developments, the restricted housing supply will push their property values higher.

As you can see, buying a house is not a purely personal decision. It already involves choices, including ethical choices that affect many people and are affected by many factors. Nor is buying a house a matter merely of participating in a pure market system. Rather, our housing systems are shaped to an amazing degree by political intervention.

THE GOVERNMENT, DEVELOPERS, AND HOUSING MARKETS

In the early twentieth century, the US government came to see homeownership as a key to a stable society. The federal government created several supporting institutions and subsidies for homeownership. First, in the 1930s, the Federal Housing Administration (FHA) began to insure loans so that banks would be willing to write longer mortgages with smaller down payments. Government-sponsored enterprises Fannie Mae and Freddie Mac were created to support the mortgage industry. Fannie Mae and Freddie Mac buy mortgages from lenders, freeing them to make more loans. The federal tax code also offers important supports for homeownership. The exemption of houses from most capital gains taxes is a huge boon for homeowners and house flippers alike. Historically, the largest subsidy in the US federal income tax code has been the mortgage interest and property tax deductions for homeowners.

Because their house is their largest financial asset, homebuyers want assurance that the character of their neighborhood won't change. Developers figured out a way to offer this assurance by adding covenants to house deeds. In the early twentieth century, many neighborhoods had covenants banning selling or renting to African Americans. For example, the Levittown communities discussed in chapter 6 had covenants prohibiting sales to African Americans. Other covenants targeted Jews, Asians, and other minority groups.

While restrictive covenants were private agreements, they depended on the courts for enforcement. Thus, the government played a key role in housing segregation. This was not the federal government's only contribution to segregation. The FHA's 1935 lending manual for banks encouraged covenants that would keep out minorities and lower-income groups. Thus, race and class segregation became a requirement of federal lending. The federal government also produced maps evaluating the security of loans made in different neighborhoods. The maps coded prime neighborhoods in green, risky ones in red. Neighborhoods with factories, poor-quality housing, and/or African Americans were "red-lined" and denied loans.

In 1948, the Supreme Court ruled that courts could no longer enforce racial covenants. Doing so would violate the equal protection clause of the Fourteenth Amendment. In response, racial discrimination took on more subtle forms. Developers switched to covenants and restrictions focused on the look of a neighborhood. Architectural standards and minimum house size requirements, for example, kept out lower-cost houses and lower-status neighbors. Real estate agents regularly steered homebuyers into neighborhoods based on their skin color. Mortgage lenders pushed African Americans into subprime loans when they could have qualified for conventional loans. Some real estate search websites gave users race and ethnicity data for neighborhoods. Other real estate websites suggested where to search for houses based on matching racial demographics to users' current neighborhoods.

Efrem Smith is a well-known pastor and author who, like me, grew up in south Minneapolis in the 1970s and 1980s. Smith, however, is African American. When his family tried to look at houses for sale in a nicer part of the city, they ran into closed doors. Real estate agents would tell them that the properties they wanted to see were no longer available. Smith's experience reminds us that "good places" can become places of conflict, where some are welcomed and others are excluded.

Local governments also fostered inequality. Cities and suburbs passed zoning laws that set aside vast areas for detached, single-family houses. Zoning laws were invented in the early twentieth century to give middle-class homeowners and their lenders confidence that nuisance uses wouldn't be allowed nearby. At the time, the greatest fear was factories being built in residential areas. Zoning was upheld in a landmark 1924 Supreme Court case, *The Village of Euclid, Ohio v. Ambler Realty*. The court ruled that zoning was a legitimate use of local government police powers. Specifically, the Village of Euclid, a suburb of Cleveland, was allowed to set aside zones dedicated to single-family housing. These residential zones were legally protected against intrusions of industry, retail, and apartments. The court agreed with Euclid's lawyers that even apartments could detract from the residential character of neighborhoods and in the wrong locations could be considered nuisances.

When zoning maps are being created, neighborhood character and property values reign supreme. Thus, single-family zoning dominates our cities and suburbs. A single-family house can be a great place of shelter, hospitality, and self-expression. But it also can be very inefficient. It consumes a wasteful amount of land and resources, and it doesn't meet the needs of certain households, such as those made up of singles and the elderly. Nonetheless, despite an intense housing crunch, Seattle, for instance, has zoned 81 percent of its residential land area for detached, single-family houses. Such zoning practices severely restrict more affordable options, such as duplexes or apartments.

Many communities go further, imposing minimum lot size requirements that keep out modestly priced single-family houses. Often, large lot zoning is rationalized by so-called environmental concerns. For example, many exclusive suburbs require two- to five-acre lot minimums to maintain a "rural" feel. This zoning may not help the environment much, but it does keep out lower-cost housing. When the Supreme Court upheld Euclid's zoning laws, the fear was that apartments might block light and bring traffic congestion. Zoning ordinances were justified to protect the community's health, safety, and welfare. But the concept of public welfare has been stretched beyond recognition. Through zoning laws, the police powers of local government are now being used to keep out affordable housing.

In established neighborhoods, homeowners often band together to fight new development. They may stage "not in my backyard" (NIMBY) protests to stop new roads, transit lines, apartments, or trailer parks. NIMBY protests focus on threats to neighborhood character and house values. Even in cities with housing shortages, single-family homeowners resist much-needed new construction. Together with zoning rules, building regulations, and permitting delays, NIMBY protests drive up housing costs for newcomers. By acting like a cartel, homeowners hoard the American Dream. And as Lee Hardy explains in *The Embrace of Buildings*, zoning rules often outlaw the dense, human-scale, mixed-use, walkable urban spaces that many of us treasure.

Government-funded affordable housing programs address only some of the gaps in our housing systems. For the lowest-income families, there are publicly owned housing units and housing choice (section 8) vouchers. Another program is the Low-Income Housing Tax Credit, which funds private sector construction of housing for low-income households. However, all of these programs put together are insufficient to meet the needs. In Kent County, Michigan, home to Grand Rapids, 12,600 housing units benefit from various government affordable housing programs. That sounds like a lot. But it is just 5 percent of the total housing stock. In Grand Rapids, the wait time for affordable housing vouchers is several years. Just getting on the wait list involves applying during a narrow window of time and getting lucky in the computerized lottery.

WHAT COULD BE WRONG?

There is no denying that our existing housing systems work well for many. Most Americans enjoy spacious housing that is the envy of the world. But sadly, our housing systems produce rather uneven results. Zoning rules combine with the vast size of new subdivisions to produce entire neighborhoods segregated by age and fine distinctions in income. When housing segregation interacts with metropolitan fragmentation (see chapter 3), the result is an unjust distribution of opportunity.

Nothing motivates NIMBY protesters like the threat of subsidized apartment projects. As a consequence, affordable and subsidized rentals are built where resistance is minimal—in existing poor neighborhoods. Thus, government programs to provide housing for the poor often end up reinforcing existing segregation.

Consider the independent suburb of East Grand Rapids, which is bordered by the city of Grand Rapids on three sides. East Grand Rapids has the most highly educated adult population in all of Michigan. Its public schools are some of the very best in the state. But who can access such educational opportunity? Almost all of East Grand Rapids is zoned for detached, single-family houses. Only a miniscule amount of land is zoned for multifamily dwellings, and they cannot exceed two stories. Demand is strong and prices are among the highest in the region. And in East Grand Rapids, there is not a single unit of subsidized low-income housing. In neighboring Grand Rapids, there are almost seven thousand units of subsidized housing. In East Grand Rapids public schools, 4 percent of students qualify for a free or reduced-price lunch, compared to 78 percent in the neighboring Grand Rapids school district. Similarly, none of the region's other top-rated school districts have any subsidized housing within their boundaries.

Housing is both a human necessity and a commodity that is bought and sold. Our housing systems are not the product of pure market forces. They are shaped by developers and banks but also by government policies. Our housing systems create a rich buffet of choices. But far too many are left behind. Good places are welcoming to all, regardless of income, age, or color. Good places need space for renters as well as homeowners. In chapter 8, we will explore ways to ensure that everyone has a good place to call home.

A Place
to Call Home

8

They will build houses and dwell in them;
they will plant vineyards and eat their fruit.

ISAIAH 65:21

TRUE HOSPITALITY

When have you experienced true hospitality? One summer while I was away on a two-week trip to Guatemala, my wife decided to take our kids to visit her parents, a day's drive away. Halfway home, our car suffered total engine failure. Stuck on the roadside with two tired kids, my wife called a nearby family member. She asked for a ride and a place to spend the night. The family member didn't want to help. Desperate, my wife called some Christian friends who lived fifty miles away. These friends had five kids of their own, including one undergoing leukemia treatments. And on that particular night, they were hosting five cousins from out of town. Nonetheless, they quickly volunteered to help. The twelve kids had an impromptu sleepover and a memorable night watching Scooby-Doo cartoons. My family spent several days at the friend's house while my wife tracked down a used engine and arranged for repairs. Under the roof of our friend's modest, one-hundred-year-old house, my wife and kids felt safe and at home.

Christian families are often extraordinarily hospitable in their homes. But sometimes our society's housing systems are not so hospitable. Too many people lack a safe and affordable place to lay their heads at night. Cultivating good places means ensuring that everyone has a good place to call home. In this chapter, we will explore solutions to housing problems. Faith-based groups have been leaders in filling gaps in our housing systems, so we will pay particular attention to their work.

HOUSING MARKETS AND CHRISTIAN CALLINGS

The Scriptures paint a complicated picture of houses. While settled, agrarian life was the Old Testament norm, Jesus described himself as lacking even a den or a nest to call his own. In Jesus's parables, houses symbolize the foundations on which we build our lives. Houses can become idols. The Scriptures sternly warn those who build bigger barns or add house to house while neglecting God and the poor. But the New Testament also contains several references to churches that met in private homes. Houses can be places where we practice the spiritual gift of hospitality. Whether we are raising children, welcoming strangers, or hosting a home fellowship group, houses are essential settings for Christian hospitality.

For American Christians, cultivating good places is easiest to envision at home in a single-family house with a private garden. According to one history of urban planning, evangelical Christians were among the founders of the contemporary suburb. In eighteenth-century London, William Wilberforce and his friends built suburban estates outside London to provide their families a quiet, domestic setting away from the temptations of the city. There the idyllic suburban house provided a suitable location for raising children and hosting friends.

But could a conflict emerge between the house as domestic refuge and store of wealth and our call to follow Christ in seeking justice and showing hospitality to the stranger? Imagine a low-income apartment building is proposed for an empty lot close to your house. Your neighbors fear it will increase traffic and crime and lower property values. Whether or not their predictions are correct, you must admit that the new apartment building will change the feel of your neighborhood. Does your call to be a good steward of your financial resources compel you to resist threats to your property value? Should you support your existing neighbors and join their NIMBY protests? Or does the call to hospitality extend to potential neighbors who might someday live in the proposed building? As we take up the task of making good places, we must always ask, "Who are these good places for?" and "Will this be a better place primarily for me and people like me or will it also be a better place for people who are quite different?"

WE CAN DO BETTER

Housing is a building block for human flourishing. To cultivate good places, we must ensure that everyone is well housed. That means we must rebalance our housing systems. Human needs must come first, profits and property values second. Put differently, we should not let the market value of housing overshadow its other values.

In many cities, people in low-wage jobs are unable to afford suitable housing. When the market fails to meet the needs of the working poor, we need to create alternatives. Solutions might take the form of real estate investors who are motivated by social concerns and are willing to take a lower rate of return. They might take the form of nonprofit housing organizations that rely on donations, volunteer labor, tax credits, and state and local incentives to make projects work. Solutions might rely on policy reform at city hall that removes barriers to affordable housing. In some locations, solutions might take the form of incentives for developers to build affordable housing.

Christian ministries are leaders in providing affordable housing. In my home of Grand Rapids, Michigan, there are three major faith-based nonprofit housing providers. Dwelling Place was founded by seven Grand Rapids churches in 1980. It operates eleven hundred affordable apartments in twenty-five buildings. The Inner City Christian Federation states that "God has called us to seek justice in our community . . . that others may see His love in action." Their work benefits over two thousand low- to moderate-income families each year. Habitat for Humanity, which has local chapters working in all fifty states and about seventy countries, is the third provider.

Habitat for Humanity grew out of the Christian convictions of its founders. Habitat for Humanity's partnership housing model offers an innovative solution where markets fail to provide affordable housing. Habitat provides housing to qualifying low- to moderate-income families through thirty-year zero interest loans and sweat equity. In 2017, the local chapters of Habitat for Humanity built over thirty-two hundred houses across the United States. That makes it the eighteenth largest homebuilder in the United States.

GOOD, AFFORDABLE HOUSING IN EVERY COMMUNITY

Christians should continue their fabulous work of providing affordable nonmarket housing. But we also need to ask why our existing market systems fail to do their job. Why is affordable housing missing from so many communities? Perhaps you have volunteered on a Habitat for Humanity house. Think about its location. Was it in a desirable part of the city? Was it located in a high-performing school district? New construction of affordable housing tends to be concentrated in lower-income communities. These places offer fewer educational and employment opportunities.

So to truly create good places, we need to insist that all communities have affordable housing.

Christians excel in showing hospitality at home. We also need to work on expressing hospitality outside the home. We need neighborhoods, zoning codes, housing systems, and public spaces that are welcoming to all. The next chapter offers suggestions for ways to engage in creating good places for all.

Toward Good
Places for All

9

They will rebuild the ancient ruins
and restore the places long devastated;
they will renew the ruined cities
that have been devastated for generations.

ISAIAH 61:4

REVISITING OUR CHILDHOOD PLACES

Places leave a lasting imprint on us. Soon after moving into an older house in Saint Peter, Minnesota, we had an unexpected visitor knock on our front door. It was an elderly gentleman who drove a red Cadillac with Arizona plates and walked with a cane. When we opened the door, he explained that he had grown up in our house. He wondered if he might take a look around his childhood home.

In the opening chapter, we recalled our childhood homes and how they shaped us. Now reflect on your childhood place in light of the elements of a good place. What did you like about it? What was missing? Did you have a secure place to call home? What kinds of public spaces—streets, sidewalks, parks, trails, libraries, and public transit—did it have? How did these spaces contribute to your experience of the world? Were there clear boundaries dividing your community from other communities? Did you grow up with an awareness of good neighborhoods and bad neighborhoods?

We are called to cultivate good places for everyone, starting in the places where we live, work, and play. Good places have local administrative boundaries that break regions into manageable size units without isolating people or hoarding resources. Good places have good neighborhoods with shared spaces for a common life. Finally, good places provide everyone a safe place to call home.

As we work to cultivate good places, we must always ask, "Better for whom?" and "Better according to whom?" If we are not careful, we can easily improve our places to the point where the original residents are displaced because they can no longer afford the cost of "better" housing.

We must consider people's ability to shape their places. Developers and affluent homebuyers have the financial resources to remake places in their own image. University-educated professionals can navigate complex city planning documents and procedures. Those who have been to university are more likely to be comfortable with public speaking. Thus, their values and visions will rise to the top in public hearings. The voices of those with less education may never be heard. Truly good places are created only when everyone has a voice in their creation.

The problems discussed in this book are deep. They are woven into the very fabric of our communities. Our places are created through processes filled with potential conflicts. The topics in this book—borders, parks, streets, transit, and housing—affect everyone's daily life. Our finances and our property values are also at stake. Seemingly mundane local government decisions, such as approving or rejecting a proposed apartment building, matter. Such decisions affect where kids go to school, where property taxes flow, and who gets to live where. Equally important are the actions of real estate agents, developers, lenders, and business owners. Sometimes these conflicts surface in local elections or public meetings. But often the conflicts remain hidden. For example, growing up in Minneapolis, I didn't see the racial discrimination that kept it from being a good place for minorities. I didn't realize that Efrem Smith's family could not buy the house they wanted and could afford.

Solutions can seem impossible because they involve sacrifice on the part of those for whom our housing, zoning, and transportation systems work pretty well. I am convinced that resources to address these problems can be found in the Christian church. The church is not, however, a social service or an urban planning agency. It is a community that gathers to worship the risen Christ, through whom God is reconciling to himself all things (Col. 1:20). Its members are being transformed by the love of Christ, in whom "there is neither Jew nor Gentile, neither slave nor free" (Gal. 3:28). The next paragraphs offer practical steps for both individuals and churches, empowered by the love of God, to cultivate good places.

NAVIGATING OUR DIVIDES

Sometimes it is easier to do short-term mission trips across international borders than to bridge the boundaries closer to home. To navigate our local political divides, we must get to know our place. We need to explore. Visit parks, stores, restaurants, and churches in neighborhoods you normally bypass. As you travel around, pay attention to the differences. Become a diligent reader of your local newspapers. Study census data and maps.

Every community has its economic divides. Many have clear racial divisions. Study your local administrative boundaries. Irregular shapes and gerrymandered lines are usually signs that the lines have been contested. It probably means that it matters which side of the line you are on. Most troubling are administrative boundary lines that trace a community's economic and racial divisions.

Loving our neighbors means becoming better informed citizens. Research your local public schools. Are there differences in the number of children who qualify for free lunches? Are there differences in graduation rates? College attendance rates? What options are open to children living in poor-performing school districts? How are local governments funded in your state? Are there differences between communities in their financial resources?

Earlier we mentioned the remarkable cooperation and resource sharing among Minneapolis, St. Paul, and their suburbs. It turns out that one of the primary forces behind that collaboration was a devout evangelical Christian named Verne Johnson. Johnson was a Republican who represented Minneapolis in the Minnesota legislature. He was passionate about both sharing the Christian faith with young people and ensuring that they had good opportunities. He led a study group that developed the set of recommendations adopted by the Minnesota legislature aimed at promoting the common good for the entire region.

We now live in an era of deepening divisions. Planners in the Minneapolis–St. Paul region doubt that their region's cooperative and resource sharing arrangements could be re-created in today's hostile climate. What hope, then, is there for bridging our entrenched divides? For Christians, the local church is a natural place to begin crossing society's dividing lines. Local congregations are places where we work out what it means to follow Christ in community. This intimate, home-away-from-home community can build the kinds of relationships that transcend boundaries of race, class, and place and form the strong bonds needed to bridge divides.

Does your congregation reflect the economic and racial diversity of your region? If not, perhaps it should develop a partnership with a church with different strengths and different demographics. Partnerships between city and suburban churches are often most successful when focused on addressing specific issues. Church partnerships can give members experiences in worshiping, fellowshiping, and working alongside believers from different backgrounds. These relationships can form a foundation for addressing more challenging issues.

RECLAIMING THE PUBLIC REALM

Public spaces have changed dramatically over the past hundred years. Public spaces belonging to everyone are less common. Travel takes place in private automobiles. Shopping takes place in privately controlled environments. Increasingly, recreation takes place within private, residents-only settings. Still, we are social beings who long for community.

Begin the work of reclamation by celebrating the public spaces in your community. Hold a church picnic in a neglected public park. Take your family swimming at the public pool. Be a tourist in your own hometown. Attend public concerts and festivals. We need shared destinations like parks, but we also need ways to get there. Those of us who use a car for all our trips need to imagine life in a wheelchair, on bike, on foot, or on public transit. I wish all drivers would commit to using public transit for one week. Then they should share what they learned and advocate for change. I am afraid they would discover that much of their city is off-limits, that waiting times are too long on weekends, that bus stops are far from store entrances, and that shelters are unheated in winter.

We must speak out when our systems fail to meet the needs of all. When we push for good public transit or safe routes for bicycles and pedestrians, we are doing it on behalf of the least among us. When serving as a decision-maker, church council member, or citizen, we must speak out for stores, offices, and churches that are accessible for those with mobility limitations or without cars.

As Christians, we can draw inspiration from the way Christian values were once inscribed into cathedral squares, village commons, and other public spaces. A good starting place for reclaiming the public realm is with our church properties. Churches, especially megachurches, have vast land holdings. We should reimagine church properties as quasi-public spaces. Church properties can be put to public use as community centers, community gardens, arts spaces, or recreational spaces. Opening church spaces to public uses can bridge the divide between the community of believers and the wider city. Some churches have converted lawns into community gardens and built connections with their neighbors. River Rock Bible Church in Austin, Texas, invited community members to design a disc golf course on a steep ravine on their property. They ended up welcoming the demographic group—young adult males—they had had the hardest time attracting.

HOUSING FOR ALL

Safe, affordable houses provide a setting for people to grow and flourish. All of us should find a way to join the wonderful work of faith-based housing providers. The hands-on work of these nonprofit organizations puts them in touch with real needs. Ask them how long the waiting list is for affordable housing in your community. Find out where new affordable housing is available and where it is missing.

Digging deeper, explore the housing choices in your city. Start in your own neighborhood. Are there housing options available so that three generations of an extended family could all find housing within walking distance of each other? Does your neighborhood have housing suited for a newly married couple on a starter income, an elderly widow who uses a walker, and a two-parent household with a bunch of young children? If not, what would need to change? Think of the service workers you encounter in your daily life. Could they afford housing in your neighborhood? What would it take so they could live close to their workplace?

Zoning, as described in chapter 7, was justified to promote the health, safety, and welfare of the community. Find out the zoning for your block. What type of buildings and uses would and would not be allowed? Would your local zoning code allow a modest Habitat for Humanity house to be built nearby? Could a duplex or four-unit apartment building be built on your street? Are there unnecessary rules or requirements that drive up the cost of housing? If you discover problems, apply to serve on your local city planning commission. There you can be a voice for change.

The church has both resources and motivations that can unblock some of the barriers to meeting housing needs. Churches have volunteers inspired by the love and hospitality of God. Churches own land throughout each metropolitan region. Some churches have partnered directly with faith-based affordable housing providers to offer financial support, volunteer time, mentoring, and even land for affordable housing projects. In the Grand Rapids region, a suburban congregation has partnered with the Inner City Christian Federation to convert part of their parking lot into an affordable housing complex. Such projects give churches the opportunity to show Christ's love in a tangible way and have a regular presence in people's lives.

AWAITING THE COMING KINGDOM

Even as we work to cultivate good places, we are bound to recognize the vast gulf between our communities and the heavenly Jerusalem. Out best-laid plans will fall short and have unintended consequences. Nonetheless, our efforts will serve as signposts of the truly good place that Christ will someday bring. In the meantime, working toward God's coming kingdom will nurture in us the heavenly virtues of faith, hope, and love.

Notes

Series Editor's Foreword

7 *Midway along the journey of our life:* The opening verse of Dante Alighieri, *The Inferno*, trans. Mark Musa (Bloomington: Indiana University Press, 1995), 19.

8 **"We are always on the road":** From Calvin's thirty-fourth sermon on Deuteronomy (5:12–14), preached on June 20, 1555 (*Ioannis Calvini Opera quae supersunt Omnia*, ed. Johann-Wilhelm Baum et al. [Brunsvigae: C. A. Schwetschke et Filium, 1883], 26.291), as quoted in Herman Selderhuis, *John Calvin: A Pilgrim's Life* (Downers Grove, IL: InterVarsity, 2009), 34.

8 **"a gift of divine kindness":** From the last chapter of John Calvin, *Institutes of the Christian Religion, 1541 French Edition*, trans. Elsie Anne McKee (Grand Rapids: Eerdmans, 2009), 704. Titled "Of the Christian Life," the entire chapter is a guide to wise and faithful living in this world.

Chapter 1

17 **It turns out, for example:** Raj Chetty, John Friedman, Nathaniel Hendren, Maggie R. Jones, and Sonya Porter, "The Opportunity Atlas: Mapping the Childhood Roots of Social Mobility," United States Census Bureau, October 2018, https://opportunityinsights .org/wp-content/uploads/2018/10/atlas_summary.pdf.

18 **You can view the online Opportunity Atlas:** See
www.opportunityatlas.org. For Canadian maps, see Miles
Corak, "Divided Landscapes of Economic Opportunity: The
Canadian Geography of Intergenerational Income Mobility,"
Working Paper 2017-043, Human Capital and Economic
Opportunity Global Working Group, University of Chicago,
May 2017, http://humcap.uchicago.edu/RePEc/hka/wpaper
/Corak_2017_Divided_Landscapes.pdf.

19 **The voting patterns of residents:** R. Alan Walks, "The Causes
of City-Suburban Political Polarization? A Canadian Case
Study, *Annals of the Association of American Geographers*
96, no. 2 (2006): 390–414; and R. Alan Walks, "Electoral
Behaviour Behind the Gates: Partisanship and Political Partici-
pation Among Canadian Gate Community Residents, *Area* 42,
no. 1 (2010): 7–24.

Chapter 2

28 **As Lutheran theologian Edgar Carlson:** This was a favorite
saying of Dr. Edgar M. Carlson, president of Gustavus Adol-
phus College from 1944 to 1968. Cited in Rod Anderson,
"Jubilee, Proclaiming the Year of the Lord's Favor," Christmas in
Christ Chapel Program (Saint Peter, MN: Gustavus Adolphus
College, 2012).

30 **Those Christians with financial means:** Bruce Winter, *Seek
the Welfare of the City: Christians as Benefactors and Citizens*
(Grand Rapids: Eerdmans, 1994).

33 **The ministries that are part:** Visit the website of the Christian
Community Development Association at www.ccda.org/.

33 **Another group, the Evangelical Environmental Network:**
Visit their website at www.creationcare.org/.

33 **The Congress for the New Urbanism:** Visit their website at
www.cnu.org/.

33 Within the CNU: Visit the website of the CNU Members Christian Caucus at www.center4eleadership.org/cnu -members-christian-caucus/.

Chapter 3

37 "Before I built a wall I'd ask to know": Robert Frost, *North of Boston* (London: David Nutt, 1914), 12. In the public domain.

38 While Flint was making dangerous: Anna Clark, *The Poisoned City: Flint's Water and the American Urban Tragedy* (New York: Metropolitan Books, 2018).

38 And as if to prove the point: Chastity Pratt, "Flint Township Tells the World: Please, Don't Confuse Us with Flint," Bridge, June 6, 2018, https://www.bridgemi.com/michigan-govern-ment/flint-township-tells-world-please-dont-confuse-us -flint.

42 Brookline, however, was home to many: Kenneth T. Jackson, *Crabgrass Frontier: The Suburbanization of the United States* (New York: Oxford University Press, 1985), 149.

43 In the fast-growing Atlanta region: Brentin Mock, "Atlanta's Cityhood Movement Might Be Out of Control," CityLab, April 16, 2018, https://www.citylab.com/equity/2018/04/atlantas -cityhood-movement-might-be-out-of-control/557993/.

43 Critics point out that the boundaries: Leora Waldner and Russell M. Smith, "The Great Defection: How New City Clusters Form to Escape County Governance," *Public Adminis-tration Quarterly* 39, no. 2 (2015): 170–219.

Chapter 4

47 "Something there is that doesn't love": Frost, *North of Bos-ton*, 12.

47 As Thomas Jefferson envisioned them: Thomas Jefferson, Letter to John Adams, October 28, 1813, in Paul Leicester Ford, ed., *The Works of Thomas Jefferson, Vol. 11 (Correspondence and Papers 1808–1816)* (New York: G. P. Putnam's Sons, 1905), https://oll.libertyfund.org/titles/807#Jefferson_0054 -11_308.

48 **He favored metropolitan regions divided:** Charles Tiebout, "A Pure Theory of Local Expenditures," *Journal of Political Economy* 64, no. 5 (1956): 416–24.

49 **Subsidiarity emphasizes that issues:** The principle of subsidiarity appears in Pope Pius XI's papal encyclical *Quadragesimo Anno* (1931), http://www.vatican.va/content/pius-xi/en /encyclicals/documents/hf_p-xi_enc_19310515_quadragesimo -anno.html, and John Paul II's papal encyclical *Centesimus Annus* (1991), http://www.vatican.va/content/john-paul-ii/en /encyclicals/documents/hf_jp-ii_enc_01051991_centesimus -annus.html.

51 **This under-bounded city lost:** Calculated by author based on US Census Bureau, "1950 Census of Population: Volume 1, Number of Inhabitants," Missouri, table 3, https://www2.census.gov /library/publications/decennial/1950/population-volume-1/vol -01-28.pdf; and US Census Bureau, "2017 American Community Survey 1-Year Estimates," Total Population, retrieved from https://factfinder.census.gov/faces/nav/jsf/pages/index.xhtml.

51 **Saint Louis residents have median household incomes:** Calculated by author based on US Census Bureau, "2013–2017 American Community Survey 5-Year Estimates," Median Household Income in the Past 12 Months, retrieved from https://factfinder.census.gov/faces/nav/jsf/pages/index.xhtml.

53 **But study after study of fragmented metropolitan regions:** Jefferey M. Sellers, Erika R. Petroy, and Sasha Hondagneu-Messner, "Contested Metropolis: Inequality and the Multilevel Governance of Metropolitan Regions in the USA," in *Inequality and Governance in the Metropolis*, ed. Jefferey M. Sellers, Marta Arretche, Daniel Kübler, and Eran Razin (London: Palgrave

Macmillian, 2017), 27-56; David Miller, Rowan Miranda, Robert Roque, and Charles Wilf, "The Fiscal Organization of Metropolitan Areas: The Allegheny Case Reconsidered, *Publius* 25, no. 4 (1995): 19–35; and Michael N. Danielson and Julian Wolpert, "Rapid Metropolitan Growth and Community Disparities," *Growth and Change* 23, no. 4 (1992): 494–515.

53 **And in the early 2000s:** *A Review of Michigan's Local Financial Emergency Law*, Michigan State University Extension, Center for Local Government Finance and Policy, April 21, 2017, https://www.canr.msu.edu/uploads/resources/pdfs/michigan_em_law_review.pdf.

56 **Fragmentation plays a role because it leads:** Richard Thompson Ford, "The Color of Territory: How Laws and Borders Keep America Segregated," in *Justice and the American Metropolis*, ed. C. R. Hayward and T. Swanstrom (Minneapolis: University of Minnesota Press, 2011), 223-236.

Chapter 5

61 **"The street, the square, the park":** Quoted in Jay Walljasper, *The Great Neighborhood Book: A Do-It-Yourself Guide to Placemaking* (Gabriola, BC: New Society Publishers, 2007), 44.

62 **As T. S. Eliot asked:** T. S. Eliot, "Choruses from 'The Rock,'" in *The Complete Poems and Plays, 1909–1950* (New York: Harcourt, Brace and World, Inc., 1971), 101.

69 **The tragic death of Buffalo, New York, teenager:** Lynne Duke, "Buffalo Family Seeking Millions for Fatal Lack of Bus Stop: Trial Centers on Teenager's Death Crossing Highway to Mall," *Washington Post*, November 15, 1999, A03.

Chapter 6

77 **"The house itself is of minor importance":** Clarence Stein to Alfred K. Stern, September 15, 1930, Presidential

Papers Subject File—Better Homes, Box 74, Herbert Hoover Presidential Library, cited in Marc A. Weiss, *The Rise of the Community Builders* (New York: Columbia University Press, 1987), 2.

79 Robert Simon planned and built: Tom Grubisich, "Reston, Virginia," in *Encyclopedia Virginia*, 2012, http://www.EncyclopediaVirginia.org/Reston_Virginia.

80 Houses in neighborhoods with HOAs: Margaret Kohn, *Brave New Neighborhoods: The Privatization of Public Space* (New York: Routledge, 2004), 90.

81 Across the United States, about 15 percent: Calculated by author based on US Census Bureau, "American Housing Survey," 2017, https://www.census.gov/programs-surveys/ahs/data/legacy/data-tools/ahstablecreator.html.

82 The New Urbanist movement recognizes: Andres Duany, Elizabeth Plater-Zyberk, and Jeff Speck, *Suburban Nation: The Rise of Sprawl and the Decline of the American Dream* (New York: North Point Press, 2010), 4-5.

82 New Urbanists call for houses set close together: Lee Hardy, *The Embrace of Buildings* (Grand Rapids: Calvin College Press, 2018), 78.

82 They have even influenced the US Department of Housing: Rebecca Sohmer and Robert Lang, "From Seaside to Southside: New Urbanism's Quest to Save the Inner City," *Housing Policy Debate* 11, no. 4 (2000): 751–60.

83 Many of the leading New Urbanist communities: Dan Trudeau and Patrick Malloy, "Suburbs in Disguise? Towards a Geography of the New Urbanism," *Urban Geography* 32, no. 3 (2011): 424–47.

83 But too often it is reduced to an aesthetic style: Sohmer and Lang, "From Seaside to Southside," 751-760.

Chapter 7

87 Psychologist Abraham Maslow developed a theory: Abraham H. Maslow, *Motivation and Personality* (New York: Harper & Brothers, 1954).

88 In Vancouver, BC, the average house costs: Demographia International, "Housing Affordability Survey: 2019," http://www.demographia.com/dhi.pdf.

89 If the homeless population of the United States were a city: Calculated by author based on US Department of Housing and Urban Development, "2018 Annual Homeless Assessment Report to Congress," https://files.hudexchange.info/resources/documents/2018-AHAR-Part-1.pdf; and US Census Bureau, "Annual Estimates of Resident Population Change for Incorporated Places of 50,000 or More in 2017, Ranked by Percent Change: July 1, 2017 to July 1, 2018," May 2019.

90 For most families, their house is their largest store: Edward N. Wolff, "The Asset Price Meltdown and the Wealth of the Middle Class," Working Paper 18559 (Cambridge, MA: National Bureau of Economic Research, 2012).

90 A three-bedroom ranch house: calculated by author based on search results for Charlotte, Michigan, Lemmon, South Dakota, Menlo Park, California, Radcliffe, Iowa, Redwood City, California, San Jose, California, and Winnebago, Minnesota from https://www.zillow.com/.

93 The FHA's 1935 lending manual: Richard Rothstein, *The Color of Law: A Forgotten History of How Our Government Segregated America* (New York: W. W. Norton, 2017), 65.

94 Real estate agents regularly steered homeowners: Peter Christensen and Christopher Timmins, "Sorting or Steering: Experimental Evidence on the Economic Effects of Housing

Discrimination," National Bureau of Economic Research, Report No. 24826, 2018, https://www.nber.org/papers /w24826.

94 Mortgage lenders pushed African Americans: Elvin K. Wyly, Mona Atia, Holly Foxcroft, Daniel J. Hammel, and Kelly Phillips-Watts, "American Home: Predatory Mortgage Capital and Neighborhood Spaces of Race and Class Exploitation in the United States," *Geografiska Annaler Series* 88, no. 1 (2006): 105–32; and Jackelyn Hwang, Michael Hankinson, and Kreg Steven Brown, "Racial and Spatial Targeting: Segregation and Subprime Lending within and across Metropolitan Areas, *Social Forces* 93, no. 3 (2014): 1081–108.

94 When his family tried to look at houses: Efrem Smith, Evangelical Covenant Church Midwinter Worship and Communion Service, 2019, https://www.youtube.com/ watch?v=v6VXymfTVBQ&t=1857s.

95 Nonetheless, despite an intense housing crunch: Emily Badger and Quoctrung Bue, "Cities Start to Question an American Ideal: A House with a Yard on Every Lot," *New York Times,* June 18, 2019, https://www.nytimes.com/ interactive/2019/06/18/upshot/cities-across-america-ques-tion-single-family-zoning.html.

96 Together with zoning rules, building regulations, and permitting delays: Jospeh Gyourko and Raven Molloy, "Regulation and Housing Supply," in *Handbook of Regional and Urban Economics*, vol. 5B, ed. Gilles Duranton, J. Vernon Henderson, and William C. Strange (Oxford, UK: Elsevier, 2015), 1289–337.

96 And as Lee Hardy explains: Hardy, *The Embrace of Buildings*, 55.

Chapter 8

102 **The Scriptures paint a complicated picture:** See Deut. 8; Isa. 5:8; Jer. 29:4–7; Matt. 8:20; Luke 6:49; 12:13–21; Rom. 16:5; Col. 4:15.

103 **According to one history of urban planning:** Robert Fishman, *Bourgeois Utopias: The Rise and Fall of Suburbia* (New York: Basic Books, 1987), 34-38.

104 **The Inner City Christian Federation states:** Inner City Christian Federation, "About Us," https://iccf.org/about/.

105 **That makes it the eighteenth largest homebuilder:** "2017 Builder 100," Builder, https://www.builderonline.com/builder -100/builder-100-list/2017/.

Chapter 9

112 **Many have clear racial divisions:** A good resource for viewing census data is https://www.socialexplorer.com.

113 **Partnerships between city and suburban churches:** Ronald J. Sider, John M. Perkins, and Wayne L. Gordon, *Linking Arms, Linking Lives: How Urban-Suburban Partnerships Can Transform Communities* (Grand Rapids: Baker Books, 2008); and Mark T. Mulder, *Congregations, Neighborhoods, Places* (Grand Rapids: Calvin College Press, 2018).

115 **They ended up welcoming the demographic group:** Susan Bratton, *Churchscape: Megachurches and the Iconography of Environment* (Waco: Baylor University Press, 2016), 298-300.

CPSIA information can be obtained
at www.ICGtesting.com
Printed in the USA
LVHW021540040921
696974LV00015B/1484

9 781937 555412